THE AUSTRALIAN CLASSICS LIBRARY

Collected Poems of John Shaw Neilson

Introduction by Helen Hewson

General editor
Robert Dixon, University of Sydney

SYDNEY UNIVERSITY PRESS

Published 2013 by Sydney University Press
First published by Lothian Book Publishing Company Melbourne and Sydney, 1934

© Introduction by Helen Hewson 2013
© Sydney University Press 2013

The publication of this book is part of the University of Sydney Library's Australian Studies electronic texts initiative. Further details are available at setis.library.usyd.edu.au/oztexts/

Reproduction and Communication for other purposes
Except as permitted under the Act, no part of this edition may be reproduced, stored in a retrieval system, or communicated in any form or by any means without prior written permission. All requests for reproduction or communication should be made to Sydney University Press at the address below:

Sydney University Press
Fisher Library
University of Sydney
NSW Australia 2006
Email: sup.info@sydney.edu.au

National Library of Australia Cataloguing-in-Publication Data

Title:	Collected poems of John Shaw Neilson / by John Shaw Neilson; introduction by Helen Hewson; general editor Robert Dixon
ISBN:	9781743320334 (pbk)
	9781743320341 (ebook: epub)
Series:	Australian classics library.
Subjects:	Australian poetry.
Other authors / contributors:	Hewson, Helen; Dixon, Robert, editor.
Dewey Number:	A821.2

Front cover image: portrait of John Shaw Neilson, 1934 (Julian Smith). Courtesy of the Mitchell Library, State Library of NSW
Cover design by Miguel Yamin

Index to Titles

John Shaw Neilson: Songs of Love and Loss, Helen Hewson	vii
Introduction, R.H. Croll	xli
All the World's a Lolly-Shop	72
Along a River	18
April Weather	128
As Far as My Heart Can Go	42
At a Lowan's Nest	21
At the End of Spring	85
The Ballad of Remembrance	172
The Bard and the Lizard	166
The Birds Go By	115
The Blue Wren in the Hop-Bush	127
Break of Day	28
The Child Being There	143
Child of Tears	55
The Child We Lost	66
Colour Yourself for a Man	131
Dear Little Cottage	48
Dolly's Offering	97
The Dream Is Deep	88
The Eleventh Moon	102
The Evening Is the Morning	104
The Eyes of Little Charlotte	31
The Flight of the Weary	139

For a Child	87
For a Little Girl's Birthday	94
From a Coffin	71
The Gentle Water Bird	176
The Girl with the Black Hair	38
The Good Season	158
Green Lover	118
Green Singer	2
Greeting	7
Half a Life Back	148
Heart of Spring!	1
The Hen in the Bushes	133
Her Eyes	43
He Sold Himself to the Daisies	144
His Love Was Burned Away	92
The Hour Is Lost	44
The Hour of the Parting	81
Inland Born	62
In the Dim Counties	107
In the Street	53
The Irish Welcome	130
It Is the Last	74
Julie Callaway	19
The Lad Who Started Out	149
Lament for Early Buttercups	147
The Land Where I Was Born	8
Little White Girl	52
Love in Absence	142
The Lover Sings	36
Love's Coming	35
The Loving Tree	59
The Luckless Bard to the Flying Blossom	70
Maggie Tulliver	26
The Magpie in the Moonlight	114
May	25

Meeting of Sighs	33
The Moon Was Seven Days Down	135
Native Companions Dancing	152
Old Granny Sullivan	22
Old Nell Dickerson	14
Old Violin	34
The Orange Tree	105
Out to the Green Fields	117
Pale Neighbour	11
Petticoat Green	4
The Petticoat Plays	57
The Poor, Poor Country	162
The Quarrel with the Neighbour	89
Ride Him Away	112
Roses Three	50
The Sacrifice	51
The Scent o' the Lover	83
Schoolgirls Hastening	96
Sheedy Was Dying	29
Show Me the Song	109
The Soldier Is Home	160
The Song and the Bird	82
Song Be Delicate	3
Song for a Honeymoon	168
So Sweet a Mouth Had She	146
Stephen Foster	153
The Stolen Lament	154
Stony Town	122
The Sun Is Up	10
Surely God Was a Lover	45
The Sweetening of the Year	116
Those Shaded Eyes	125
'Tis the White Plum Tree	99
To a Blue Flower	13
To a Lodging-House Canary	151

To an Early-Flowering Almond	124
To a Schoolgirl	98
'Twas in the Early Summer Time	40
Under a Kurrajong	69
The Unlovely Player	100
The Wedding in September	78
When Kisses Are as Strawberries	95
The White Flowers Came	76
The Whistling Jack	155
The Winter Sundown	164
The Woman of Ireland	110
You, and Yellow Air	46

John Shaw Neilson: Songs of Love and Loss

Helen Hewson

> It is of Love and lovers—all the old dream in me—
> Weary am I of Hate and Pride and its finery:
> Summer is soon behind and the Autumn stays not long:
> Is it of Love that you sing, sing, sing? Show me the song![1]

JOHN Shaw Neilson (1872–1942) is Australia's great songwriter and love poet. His unique voice compelled attention and under the guidance of three very different editors, A.G. Stephens, R.H. Croll and James Devaney, five collections of his verse were published during his lifetime. The *Collected Poems of John Shaw Neilson*, published by Thomas Lothian in 1934, is particularly significant because Robert Croll encouraged Neilson to select, correct, alter and arrange the poems he regarded as representative of his work. Neilson seized this opportunity, dealing confidently with Arthur Greening of Lothian and participating in every detail from copyright issues with A.G. Stephens' daughter, Connie Robertson, correcting insertions by his first editor, providing new stanzas, to book signings with the booksellers Robertson and Mullens, and attending a celebratory poetry reading at the bookshop of Margareta Webber. This material is contained in the papers of the

---

1   Poems cited from the *Collected Poems* are shown with the page number in brackets, e.g. 'Show Me the Song' (109).

Lothian Publishing Co. and reproduced in Helen Hewson's, *John Shaw Neilson, A Life in Letters*.[2]

A.H. Spencer, the proprietor of the Hill of Content bookshop, 96 Bourke Street, Melbourne, was also an enthusiastic supporter of the project, observing: "Neilson's turn of word or phrase is often so startlingly beautiful that one feels as in the presence of a miracle. Consider his use of 'assault' in 'The Hour of the Parting' " (81).[3] Spencer arranged for the Melbourne surgeon and renowned amateur photographer, Mr Julian Smith, to provide the portraits for Lothian's deluxe edition of the poems.[4] "He gave that night three hours of time to taking pictures of Neilson . . ." This remarkable encounter is recalled in Spencer's memoir: "One portrait exhibits to perfection the calm wisdom of the poet's facial expression . . . the other . . . the poet's rugged and worn hands . . . this farm-worker's calloused hands had written poetry so miraculous in intent and beauty as to make William Blake his brother."[5] When the *Collected Poems* was published, Neilson wrote to Croll: "I think the Printers have turned out a very nice book indeed and in Dr Smith's photos, I am quite a poetical looking old chap. The Doctor is an extraordinary man. When he is taking a picture, he is like a conductor with a choir."[6]

Neilson's selection contains some of his finest poems. 'The Gentle Water Bird' (176), 'You, and Yellow Air' (46), 'The Evening Is the Morning' (104), 'The Sun Is Up' (10), 'Song Be Delicate' (3) and 'When Kisses Are as Strawberries' (95) have appeared in anthologies[7] while others are less well-known like 'The Soldier Is Home' (160)—an exceptional poem about war, and 'The Ballad of Remembrance' (172) recalling the

---

2   Lothian Papers, The La Trobe Library, State Library of Victoria. Helen Hewson, *John Shaw Neilson, A Life in Letters*, Miegunyah, Melbourne University Press, 2001, pp. 232–68 (hereafter HH).
3   A.H. Spencer, *The Hill of Content*, Angus & Robertson, Sydney, 1959, p. 230.
4   In the standard edition of *Collected Poems* the frontispiece portrait is by Mrs Stanley Gibson, and incorrectly attributed to Stanley Gibson.
6   Neilson–R.H. Croll, 17.vi.1934, (LaT MS8910 Box 1206/4(b) RHCP); HH261.
7   *Australian Poetry Since 1788*, Geoffrey Lehmann & Robert Gray (Eds), UNSW Press, Sydney, 2011. Neilson has twenty poems in this anthology including his light verse and ten limericks.

convict days. The literary critic, Tom Inglis Moore, wrote: "the singer of 'Love's Coming' (35) and 'The Orange Tree' (105) is magician and mystic both".[8] Not surprisingly Neilson is regarded now among the finest lyric poets writing in English during the first half of the twentieth century, and his poems continue to be enjoyed and set to music by composers at home and abroad.[9]

Indeed, the composer Margaret Sutherland wrote to Neilson after reading the *Collected Poems*: "I have set some of your voice to music and should feel relieved if I could have your consent! Your new volume of collected verse enabled me to realise so vividly the musical quality of it all, and with great despatch the deed was done."[10] She listed six titles and went on to set further poems by Neilson which were published by Louise Dyer, a Melbourne patron of the arts, who founded L'Oiseau-Lyre Press and Recording Company in Paris. Neilson dedicated the *Collected Poems* to Louise Dyer in gratitude for her financing his second book *Ballad and Lyrical Poems* (1923) and her continued support and interest over many years.[11]

Neilson's collaboration with Croll has produced an excellent introduction to his poetry. His final book, *Beauty Imposes*,[12] contains a further eleven new poems, including 'The Crane Is My Neighbour', begun in 1934, which is also discussed in this essay. Since Neilson's death there have been editions of his poetry and letters, biographies, and critical assessment of his work dating from the 1940s to the present day. Most editors have drawn on the Croll edition as well as previously unpublished material and some, in the manner of A.G. Stephens, have

---

8   T. Inglis Moore, *Six Australian Poets*, Robertson & Mullen, Melbourne, 1942, pp. 62–64; HH422–23.
9   Alfred and Mirrie Hill, Moya Henderson, Alan Tregaskis, Gerald Glynn, Barry McKimm, David Morris, Darryl Emmerson, Philip Bracanin, Wilfred Holland, Horace Keats, Christopher Willcock, Graham Hair and many others.
10 Margaret Sutherland–Neilson, 19.viii.1934 (LaT LP); HH270–27.
11 Jim Davidson, 'The Neilson Ambience' in *Lyrebird Rising, Louise Hanson-Dyer of L'Oiseau-Lyre 1884–1962*, Miegunyah Press, Melbourne, 1994, pp. 63–75; Helen Hewson, 'Shaw Neilson and the Ladies' College, Melbourne', *Southerly*, Vol. 67, Nos 1–2, 2007, pp. 272–83.
12 James Devaney (Ed.), *Beauty Imposes*, Angus & Robertson, Sydney, 1938.

made alterations or rearranged verses when presenting a preferred version of a poem. This has proved a temptation and a challenge because of the extensive scholarly research into Neilson's notebooks, manuscripts, poems and correspondence that has revealed lost or forgotten lines as well as incomplete or experimental attempts. Among fragments and lengthier pieces are examples of his extraordinary imagery, flashes of humour or outrage and his moods of reflective tenderness: too good to be overlooked or rejected, even by the poet! Editorial selections are always subjective but I refer in this essay to the electronic *John Shaw Neilson, The Collected Verse—A Variorum Edition* (2003) edited by Margaret Roberts for the provenance and version of poems referred to but not included in the *Collected Poems*.[13]

The Neilsons all wrote poetry. The father, John Neilson, had verse printed in the local press and posthumously collected in book form.[14] An extract from 'The Last Time' written in 1898 following the death of his wife, Margaret, has been included in Croll's Introduction to the *Collected Poems* (xli). John Neilson's moving evocation of love and loss is very different in language and form from his son's spare and bleak poem, 'The Hour of the Parting' (81) written in 1906. This poem exhibits, as does 'The Orange Tree' (105), the change in lyric writing which evolved during the twentieth century where the poet may be emotionally subjective, or even ambivalent, posing unresolved questions, juxtaposing contrasting themes and often depicting scenes from everyday life framed in vivid, cinematic sequences as in 'Schoolgirls Hastening' (96).

* * *

---

13 Margaret Roberts (Ed.), *John Shaw Neilson, The Collected Verse*, Australian Scholarly Editions Centre UNSW at ADFA, Canberra, 2003 (hereafter MR).
14 John Neilson, *The Men of the Fifties*, Hawthorn Press, Melbourne, 1938; Andrew G. Peake (Ed.) *John Neilson, Poet and Songwriter*, Proformat, Adelaide, 2009 includes 'The Last Time', pp. 98–99.

Shaw Neilson, as he mostly signed his verse and correspondence, was born in Penola, South Australia in 1872. The eldest child of Scottish parents, he received little formal schooling and farmed with his father and younger brothers in the poor soil of the Wimmera in Victoria. When failed crops and creditors drove the family from the land, they became itinerant rural workers. 'The Poor, Poor Country' (162) describes Neilson's childhood, although in 1917, he wrote: "The land is all right if you are suited for the monotony of the land. I don't think I am."[15] Neilson suffered bouts of depression and tragic losses, the deaths of a baby brother, two sisters in their early twenties from tuberculosis and, when he was only twenty-five, that of his mother. He joined his sister Annie McKimm and her family in Melbourne in 1928 and was employed as an interdepartmental messenger with the Country Roads Board to augment a modest Commonwealth Literary Pension. He never married, and cared for his wider family until he died in 1942.[16]

The compensation for hard times was surely the social music making, singing, dancing and recitations enjoyed by a rural community of English, Gaelic, Scottish, Irish and German speakers. These pleasurable occasions are celebrated in 'The Wedding in September' (78), 'Dear Little Cottage' (48) and 'Take Down the Fiddle Karl'.[17] Other influences shaping Neilson's work were his family life, religious upbringing, his reading and participation in the writing culture of the day, as well as the rural and urban landscapes in which he lived and worked. These are considered in this essay.

Opportunities for further education through reading were available at the Penola Mechanics' Institute and, after the family crossed the border into Victoria, the free library at Nhill, satirised by Neilson in verse.[18] In addition, the family's few books were excellent literary models and well read. The greatest influence was the Authorised Version or

---

15   Neilson–Victor Kennedy, 24.vi.1917 (La. MS 9419/1237 VKP); HH71.
16   Helen Hewson, 'John Shaw Neilson' in Nicholas Jose (Gen. Ed.), *The Macquarie PEN Anthology of Australian Literature*, Allen & Unwin, Sydney 2009, pp. 311–12.
17   'Take down the Fiddle Karl' (MR1043).
18   'Our Free Library' (MR156).

King James Bible (1611), of which Coleridge believed: "Intense study ... will keep any writer from being vulgar in point of style."[19] At times Neilson seems a visionary. His poetry reveals a familiarity with the books of the Old Testament, in particular the Psalms, Proverbs, Isaiah, Ecclesiastes, Lamentations, as well as the Christian themes of love in the New Testament gospels and epistles.[20] His nephew Alan McKimm recalls: "He reckoned Paul's letters were the greatest literary things he'd ever read. '... When I was a child, I thought as a child, I spoke as a child ...' He liked that."[21]

Neilson's longing for love, pity, mercy, justice and beauty in the world is often voiced in the powerful language, of the King James Bible. Words such as "neighbour", "sober", "dim", "excellent", "instruction", "creed", "parable", "manna", "spend", "thief", "climbing", "eyelids", "honey" and "gold" are used in a context enriched by layers of meaning no longer in use today. Word pairing is part of the oral tradition of the Bible. Words can be fixed into familiar associations and when one is used the listener anticipates the other. Neilson links "honey" and "gold" frequently in his work, recalling Psalm 19.[22] In 'Song Be Delicate' (3) there are discarded stanzas which contain the lines "the touch of gold" and "Perils in gold", and these would have paired in his mind with the retained image "the bees are home: / All their day's love is sunken / Safe in the comb."

At times Neilson's imagery astonishes. For example his appropriation of the Suffering Servant from Isaiah is juxtaposed with a terrible, frowning God. The latter also appears in the hymns of Isaac Watts,

---

19   Samuel Taylor Coleridge, 'Study of the Bible', *Table Talk*, 14 June 1830.
20   See Helen Hewson, 'The Guest of the Sunlight' in Colette Rayment and Mark Levon Byrne (Eds), *Seeking the Centre*, 2001 Australian International Literature and the Arts Conference Proceedings, RLA Press, Sydney, 2002, pp. 293–304; also HH28–36.
21   Interview with Jack, Mary, Alan and Barry McKimm. Cliff Hanna, (Ed.), *John Shaw Neilson*, University of Queensland Press, St Lucia, 1991, p. 343.
22   Psalm 19:7–10 is about the Law of the Lord and his Statutes: "More to be desired are they than gold, yea, than much fine gold: sweeter also than honey and the honey comb".

William Cowper and John Newton.[23] Both images inform 'The Gentle Water Bird' (176).

> Gracious he was and lofty as a king:
> Silent he was, and yet he seemed to sing
> Always of little children and the Spring
>
> God? Did he know him? It was far he flew...
> God was not terrible and thunder-blue:
> —It was a gentle water bird I knew.
>
> Pity was on him for the weak and strong,
> All who have suffered when the days were long,
> And he was deep and gentle as a song.
>
> As a calm soldier in a cloak of grey
> He did commune with me for many a day
> Till the dark fear was lifted far away.

'The Gentle Water Bird' is a confessional poem, composed in 1924 and dedicated to Mary Gilmore. Neilson had worked on it for "over eighteen months" and it recalls an epiphany from his youth which led to his apprehension of God and "his first idea of right religion too".[24] Neilson's reassuring encounter recalls Psalm 91:4—"He shall cover thee with his feathers, and under his wings shalt thou trust: his truth shall be thy

---

23 Isaac Watts: "Now thou array'st thine awful face / In angry frowns, without a smile"—'Lord We Adore Thy Vast Designs'; William Cowper: "Behind a frowning providence / He hides a smiling face"—'God Moves in a Mysterious Way'; John Newton: "Will sinners bear to see his face, / Or stand before his frown?"—'Thunder'. Shaw Neilson: 'You with a Frown' (MR1169); 'Be at the Garden' (MR 692).
24 James Devaney, *Shaw Neilson*, Angus & Robertson, Sydney, 1944, pp. 198–99.

shield and buckler" and is drawn upon by Patrick White in *The Tree of Man*, where "the day had lulled Stan Parker into a sense of security as sure and soft as cranes' wings".[25]

The Neilsons were strict members of the Presbyterian Church, and although their Calvinistic beliefs have been regarded as detrimental, the discipline and focus on reading and listening to the Word proved beneficial to the poet as did the strong belief in congregational singing and the design of the Scottish Psalter with its metrical psalms and paraphrases transposed to the common, long and short metres of the ballad form.[26] In the absence of an organ these would be sung unaccompanied and 'lined out' for the congregation to follow. They were, Neilson responded: "Welcome as little warblings in a rhyme".[27] Naturally he absorbed the extravagant outpourings of the psalm writers' heavy, earthy and joyous poems of love between man and God, writing in his own jubilant way: "Into the wedding feast there came / The many psalms of Spring".[28] Neilson was exposed to a rich vein of poetry in the Scottish hymn-books, based on earlier English hymnals, which included the work of George Herbert, John Milton, Joseph Addison, John Whittier and Charles Wesley.

Throughout his life Neilson was often critical of the Church, recalling in a final poem: "Once in a while I sought a holy day / Out to the edge to have encouragement / But the dull moan of business led the way".[29] He told his final editor and friend, James Devaney, that as an adult he didn't follow any particular religion, didn't go to church or belong to a sect but believed in a Creator of the universe.[30] He could not understand intolerance or religious bigotry and in 'The World as a Rhyme', concluded, "I know not the Rhymer / I know but a part of his rhyme".[31] Neilson's rejection of orthodox religious instruction and the

---

25   Patrick White, *The Tree of Man*, Jonathan Cape, London, 1955, p.155.
26   A paraphrase or metaphrase in seventeenth-century Scotland meant a metrical translation.
27   'Some Thievery of Old' (1941) (MR1015).
28   'The Wedding in September' (78).
29   'Some Thievery of Old' (1941) (MR1015).
30   James Devaney, *Shaw Neilson*, Angus & Robertson, Sydney, 1944, p.6.

"arrogant" drumming of the Salvation Army campaigners in the Wimmera during the late 1880s emerges as an important theme in his work. In 'Out to the Green Fields' (117) he refers to "standing as children under a heavy psalm" and being driven "to trampling on the holy things" in 'The Sacrifice' (51), and yet he reveals an appreciation of Christ's teachings as a pattern for living and social equality. For example, in 1934, the year he was involved in the *Collected Poems*, Neilson returned to the metaphoric possibilities of the gentle water bird in 'The Crane Is My Neighbour' which was published in his final collection *Beauty Imposes* (1938), edited by James Devaney.

> The bird is my neighbour, a whimsical fellow and dim;
> There is in the lake a nobility falling on him.
>
> The bird is a noble, he turns to the sky for a theme,
> And the ripples are thoughts coming out to the edge of a dream.
>
> The bird is both ancient and excellent, sober and wise,
> But he never could spend all the love that is sent for his eyes
>
> He bleats no instruction, he is not an arrogant drummer;
> His gown is simplicity— blue as the smoke of the summer.
>
> How patient he is as he puts out his wings for the blue!
> His eyes are as old as the twilight, and calm as the dew.
>
> The bird is my neighbour, he leaves not a claim for a sigh,
> He moves as the guest of the sunlight—he roams in the sky.

---

31 'The World as a Rhyme' (MR914).

> The bird is a noble, he turns to the sky for a theme,
> And the ripples are thoughts coming out to the edge of a dream.

With the familiar cadence of "The Lord is my shepherd", "The crane is my neighbour" answers a significant question, "Who is my neighbour?"[32] The question was asked of Jesus by a young lawyer. He answered with the parable of the Good Samaritan, an example of the unconditional love also portrayed in Psalm 23. Neilson's poem has the circular structure of one of the shorter psalms of praise. After the introductory exaltation, the personification of the bird develops through the use of climactic parallelism which creates the repetitive build up of the crane. "The bird is my neighbour ... The bird is a noble ... ancient and excellent, sober and wise." Synonymous parallelism, where the same sentiment is repeated in different but equivalent terms, occurs in the lines "He bleats no instruction, he is not an arrogant drummer" and in the line where the bird as a true "neighbour", "leaves not a claim for a sigh". The poem concludes with a repetition of the theme.

Among the lines discarded by Neilson during the poem's composition are: "How cautious he is as he folds up his wings for the blue" and "The bird is a Noble he calls me to walk in the dim / I am young as the grass when / I go to my journey with him". 'The Gentle Water Bird' finishes on a similar note, "Silent—how silent—but his heart will sing / Always of little children and the Spring". Both examples recall Mark 10:15 "Whosoever shall not receive the kingdom of God as a little child, he shall not enter therein."

A final example of the positive influence of Neilson's religious upbringing on his poetry is his incorporation of the revelatory epiphany, pivotal to the shaping of 'The Orange Tree' (105) and 'In the Street' (53). Three phases are common to divine manifestation in the Bible. First, a dramatic revelation, often a fire or a bright light associated with purification. This is followed by a call or an awakening, and finally, the

---

32 Luke 10:25–37.

induction or task. Bearing this in mind Neilson's evocation "There is a light, a step, a call, / This evening on the Orange Tree" is analogous to Moses' epiphany when he discovered a burning bush that was not being consumed and from which the voice of God spoke. 'In the Street' (53) we read:

> Slowly into our hearts there crept
> I know not what: it flamed! it leapt!
> Was it God's love that in us slept? . . .
>   I saw the mark
> Of tears upon her, as she stept
>   Into the dark.

Similarly, there is an illuminating threefold awakening in 'The Poor Can Feed the Birds' where Neilson celebrates "the feast of love . . . it reigns, it calls, / It chains us to the pure".[33]

John Bunyan's robust, allegorical work *The Pilgrim's Progress* (1678) was standard reading in godly households into the twentieth century and often quoted within the Neilson family. No doubt the steadfastness of Christian and Hopeful provided encouragement during the Neilsons' own tribulations. Cherished too, and recited, was the poetry of Robert Burns, whose depiction of a humble, pious family at worship in 'The Cotter's Saturday Night'—a splendid poem of place—may not be too far removed in spirit from the Neilson household.

---

33 'The Poor Can Feed the Birds' (MR1079–1085).

> ... The priest-like father reads the sacred page
> How Abram was the friend of God on high;
> ...
> Or Job's pathetic plaint, and wailing cry;
> Or rapt Isaiah's wild, seraphic fire;
> ...
> Perhaps the Christian volume is the theme,
> How guiltless blood for guilty man was shed:
> How He, who bore in Heaven the second name,
> Had not on earth whereon to lay His head.
> ...
> Then, kneeling down to Heaven's Eternal King
> The saint, the father, and the husband prays ... [34]

D.H. Lawrence in his essay 'Hymns in a Man's Life' sums up well the relevance of early religious practices and their long-term influence on a person's view of life.

> Nothing is more difficult than to determine what a child takes in and does not take in, of its environment and its teaching. This fact is brought home to me by the hymns which I learned as a child, and never forgot ... The same with all the religious teaching I had as a child *apart* from the didactism and sentimentalism. I am eternally grateful for the wonder with which it filled my childhood.[35]

* * *

---

[34] Cited by J.A. Mackay, *The Presbyterian Way of Life*, Prentice Hall, 1960, p.161.
[35] D.H. Lawrence, 'Hymns in a Man's Life' in J.T. Boulton (Ed.), *Late Essays and Articles, The Cambridge Edition of the Works of D.H. Lawrence*, Vol. II, Cambridge University Press, Cambridge, 2004, pp. 131–34.

Neilson was always keen to see his verse in print. His first editor, the literary critic and writer A.G. Stephens, published his verse in the Red Page of the *Bulletin* and later in his literary magazine the *Bookellow*.[36] In December 1906 he invited Neilson to: "make me your agent for the disposal and publication of all literary work that you may do, and to offer me in the first instance any of your verses".[37] Neilson accepted. Stephens launched Neilson's first book, *Heart of Spring*, in 1919 presenting Neilson as "First of Australian poets"[38] and claiming:

> Lines such as "And all the sighing bloom / That takes the dew" have a touch of Shakespeare. The pure depth of his feeling recalls Blake; his verses come like Blake's children "with innocent faces clean".[39]

This was an extravagant claim to make for a newcomer to the literary scene and the critics pounced. However as Neilson's verse became known, he was introduced to, and corresponded with, some of the leading Australian writers and artists of the day. Many provided encouragement, books and practical assistance.

One enthusiast was Mary Gilmore who wrote to Neilson in 1912, after reading 'Love's Coming' (35) in the Sydney *Sun*. She sent him copies of her books and reprinted 'Marian's Child' in her exposé of 'baby farming'.[40] He discussed her poems and the articles she wrote for the women's page of the Sydney *Worker*. In their handwritten correspondence Neilson opens up both emotionally, when discussing his family's fragile health, and intellectually, when sharing his love of art and poetry and the most important element in his verse. ' "Music ever!" I think it is Verlaine says that.'[41]

---

36 Roger Osborne, "Separating the 'Bookfellow' from the *Bookfellow*: A.G. Stephens and the Australian Magazine Reader." *Script and Print*, 29 (1–4). 2005, pp. 260–75.
37 A.G. Stephens–Neilson, 7.xii.1906 (ML MSS 3354/1:1–2NFP).
38 For critical reception of Neilson's books see HH406–09.
39 William Blake, 'Holy Thursday', quoted by A.G.Stephens in Preface to *Heart of Spring*, The Bookfellow, Sydney, 1919; HH406.
40 'Marian's Child' (MR129–130).

Although it was difficult for an itinerant bush worker, Neilson tried to keep up with current writing in the press and the often short-lived arts journals such as *Birth, New Triad,* and *Verse* to which he was invited to contribute. *Heart of the Rose* with Nettie Palmer's translation of Paul Verlaine's *Art Poetique* was one of the few Neilson managed to save.[42] Verlaine's *symboliste* manifesto and pronouncement MUSIC EVER, parallels those qualities Neilson emphasises in 'Song Be Delicate' (3). Like any dedicated artist, Neilson selected intuitively from his reading, his surroundings, and life experience.

"I have Palgrave's anthology. There is plenty of poetry there," he told Gilmore.[43] *The Golden Treasury of the Best Songs and Lyrical Poems in the English Language* (1861) selected by Francis Palgrave provided Neilson with a diverse range of poetry and poetics.[44] A rich source of inspiration, beginning with Thomas Nashe's 'Spring' "when maids dance in a ring" and Shakespeare's "In the Springtime, the only pretty ring time", Palgrave clearly provided models for Neilson. Included here along with Marlowe, Drayton, Jonson and Marvell are cries of 'Cherry Ripe' from Thomas Campion and Robert Herrick, the latter bewitched by "the tempestuous petticote". In 'The Petticoat Plays' (57) it becomes Neilson's "little silk ally" in the expression of sensual love, passionate fulfilment and loss. Palgrave's inclusion of Colonel Lovelace's 'To Lucasta, On Going to the Wars' also struck a chord with Neilson. "I could not love thee dear so much / Loved I not honour more." "All our modern ranting stuff seemed pumped up after that," he asserted to Gilmore.[45] Ranging from Shakespeare to Wordsworth, one should

---

41   Neilson–Mary Gilmore, 13.ii.1921; HH91–92.
42   Nettie Palmer's English translation of Verlaine's manifesto was printed under the pseudonym "Owen Roe O'Neil" in the first issue of *The Heart of the Rose*, a literary magazine started by William Mitchell, edited by Bernard O'Dowd and published in Melbourne by Thomas Lothian in 1907. See Helen Hewson, ' "Music ever!" John Shaw Neilson's encounter with Paul Verlaine' in *Southerly*, Vol. 68, No. 3, 2008, pp. 213–27.
43   Neilson–Mary Gilmore, 26.iii.1914 (ML A3267 PDMG); HH63.
44   Lisette Noblett–Helen Hewson, 17 October 1993. "Many lovely poems. It belonged to either my mother or father." Lisette was Neilson's half-sister.
45   Neilson–Mary Gilmore, 15.xi.1915 (ML MSS123 PDMG); HH63.

not underestimate the impact this popular anthology had on early Australian writers and readers. And not only Australian writers. Thomas Hardy (1840–1928), who loved nature and also wrote longingly of past loves, commented: "I myself have been led to read poets by seeing specimens in [such] anthologies." It has been noted that Hardy's copy of *The Golden Treasury* is the most marked of the many he owned.[46]

Other influences in Neilson's writing can clearly be traced to children's games and rhymes—"the most mysterious fragments from our shared memory"[47] and to the folksongs of the British Isles, Stephen Foster's American compositions and Australian bush balladry. Importantly, Neilson picked up on aspects of the literary and visual Zeitgeist through the many illustrated magazines, the *Bulletin*, the *Lone Hand*, and art journals like *The Studio* and *Art in Australia* available in the public libraries of Melbourne and Bendigo and bookshops. Blamire Young wrote romantically about Neilson for *Art in Australia* which also published 'Song for a Honeymoon' (168) and Will Dyson's charcoal portrait of Neilson.[48] Through reading, visiting the theatre and galleries, Neilson familiarised himself with influences such as the aesthetic movement, the *Symbolistes*, the Folkloric and Celtic Twilight and the Victorian fascination with fairies and the supernatural. He was interested in the popular scientific writings of Ernst Haeckel, Joseph McCabe and others reprinted in the *Lone Hand*.[49] Any material of interest Neilson infused into his reworking of traditional themes, symbols and colours.

Neilson's early poetry was imitative in structure and subject matter. Romantic narratives illustrated innocence and experience, youth and age, loneliness or decay, as in 'Old Nell Dickerson' (14), and 'Julie Callo-

---

46 Dennis Taylor, 'Hardy's Copy of "The Golden Treasury"', *Victorian Poetry*, Vol. 37, No. 2. *Palgrave's "Golden Treasury" and Victorian Anthologies*, Summer 1999, West Virginia University Press, p. 165.
47 Iona Opie, *Mother Goose's Little Treasures*, Walker Books, London, 2007, p. 4.
48 Blamire Young, "John Shaw Neilson" and John Shaw Neilson: 'Song for a Honeymoon' in *Art in Australia*, Third Series No. 34, October–November, 1930, pp. 40–42.
49 There are a number of poems about evolution, geology and fossils, e.g. 'The Walker on the Sand' (MR1121).

way' (19). Similar themes and metre are found in the ballads of Thomas Hood, Robert Buchanan and the art songs of the Victorian drawing-room. He discovered modern writers like Francis Thompson in *Poets of Today* (1915), *The Book of Irish Poetry* (1916) and Padraic Colum's *Wild Earth* (1916). The latter's homely imagery can be seen in 'Dear Little Cottage' (48) and 'The Woman of Ireland' (110). In addition to the poetry collections received from Australian writers, European examples were provided by Stephens and Louise Dyer, and Robert Bridges the Poet Laureate, who sent poems of Hafiz translated by his wife, Elizabeth.[50]

More importantly Neilson was a nature poet living and working throughout the seasons in the Australian landscape. He describes it in 'The Flight of the Weary' (139).

> The lakes shall be many and gentle:
> The water-birds, holy and wise,
> Shall put the grief out of your shoulders
> And pull the pain out of your eyes:
> Our God shall be drowsy, and think out
> His thoughts like a beautiful tree...

Like the neighbourly crane, Neilson often searched "the sky for a theme" and birds are a persistent motif in his writing—the blue wren (127), the magpie (114), the lowan (21) and the water birds. Traditionally birds are the messengers linking heaven and earth, and in Neilson's poetry they are subject to creative transformations. From the biblical references shaping the blue crane and its message of pity and love we encounter another source. Neilson saw a London production of Maurice Maeterlinck's Fairy Play, *The Blue Bird* (1908) brought to Mel-

---

50   Robert Bridges–Neilson, 30.i.1924; HH124; Hewson, 'Shaw Neilson, Hafez and Omar Khayyam—"A Book of Verse underneath the Bough" ', the Shaw Neilson Memorial Lecture: Maribyrnong Library, Foostcray, Victoria, 14 November 2010.

bourne in 1911 by J.C. Williamson. It is about a boy and a girl who go on a quest seeking the turtle-dove which will become blue when they have discovered their full potential as kind and loving people. The play's message, emphasising the power of self-knowledge, resonates in 'The Gentle Water Bird' where God is recognised as "not terrible and thunder-blue" but is like a blue crane singing "Always of little children and the Spring".

Within a year of being introduced to *The Blue Bird*, our poet is in despair. Like one of the lovers in the play, he has been forced to say goodbye to his sweetheart. In 'The Lament for Sadie' a distraught Neilson writes:

> She is not here. She will never come.
> Why will the blue bird say to his love, I am your lover,
> All your body is mine, your voice cooing, crying?
> I am athirst with love in a white anger.
> . . .
> No lips were as red as the lips of my Sadie—
> Tear my heart out, O God, hear me! I struggle.[51]

In the last line you can hear the psalmist beseeching: "Give ear to my prayer O God / Attend unto me, and hear me: I mourn . . .". He continues desperately: "Oh that I had wings like a dove! / For then would I fly away and be at rest."[52] Years later the world-weary poet, no doubt with a twinkle in his eye dispatched *that* bird forever in a light piece of verse entitled: 'When Does a Burglar Happen to Shave' (1934). It begins: "In days when Maeterlinck's bird of blue / Told us all its garrulous fibs . . ."[53]

"How hard it is to write a song", Neilson mused in a letter to Mary Gilmore. "I should say a man would need to be twenty-one, with all good health and plenty of sunlight, but I'm wrong altogether because

---

51 'The Lament for Sadie' (MR535–36).
52 Psalm 55.
53 'When Does a Burglar Happen to Shave' (MR668).

great songs have been written by poor miserable wasters, homeless and penniless."[54] Neilson preferred to dictate much of his verse and correspondence to family or friends because of his poor eyesight; it also helped him to concentrate on ideas and rhymes. He recalled in conversation with James Devaney that during the period 1905 to 1915 he composed mostly when working on horseback. After humming a tune, he tried to make up one of his own. Unsuccessful, he would give up and tackle rhyming. After discovering a suitable stanza and working on it, he claimed to have rarely altered the verse form leaving the composition to dictate or handwrite later.[55] However the latter comment is not born out by the rewriting and unfinished attempts at verse scattered throughout Neilson's remaining exercise books and ledgers.

Toiling in the bush, or at the hard edge of a city, Neilson looked always for beauty in nature and mankind. In 1936 he wrote to James Devaney "Beauty does create in us a strange wonderment and awe." "It is difficult to describe in words the effect that a beautiful nude has upon one's feelings."[56] Neilson preferred the beauty of Botticelli's women he had seen reproduced in books, was enthusiastic about the etchings of Max Klinger at the National Gallery of Victoria although very critical of the painting of the *Madonna and Child* acquired by the Trustees in 1922.[57] "There is no beauty in the Woman's face. She seems sleepy, insipid . . .", he told Mary Gilmore.[58] Beauty could be found in the changing seasons, the birds, the flowers, or a full-eyed wallaby, and hoped for in the young.

The child as the embodiment of innocence is another motif in Neilson's writing. It is the unsoiled children who have not been fed "idle tales" and "heavy psalms" who will provide the hope for man-

---

54 Neilson–M.Gilmore, 24.xi.1918, (ML MSA 3267 V.16 PDMG); HH75–76.
55 James Devaney, *Shaw Neilson*, Angus & Robertson, pp. 11–16.
56 Neilson–J. Devaney, 20.i.1936 (NLA MS1145/33 H.F. Chaplin Coll.); HH303. See Neilson's appreciation of the arts in Helen Hewson, 'John Shaw Neilson: A Painterly Poet', *Antipodes*, Vol. 23, No. 2, December 2009, pp. 161–67.
57 After Van Eyck: *Madonna and Child*, panel 26.3 x 19.4 cm. Acquired by the National Gallery of Victoria through the Felton Bequest in 1922.
58 Neilson–Mary Gilmore, 8.iv.1923 (ML MSS123: 21–24 PDMG); HH106.

kind—"Only low with the young love the olden hates are healed" (117). In the poem 'The People in the Playground' he recognises children unspoiled by "our cures—our creeds—decrepit cold" and writes:

> See how these little people play
> Loudly as sailors lost in wine;
> Long did I watch them yesterday,
> And in their shouting sought a sign.[59]

Neilson is insightful and his watching of children at play to my mind cannot be interpreted as in any way prurient. T.S. Eliot in his First Quartet, 'Burnt Norton' (1935) writes of "a shaft of sunlight" and in this moment of illumination "There arises the hidden laughter / Of children in the foliage / Quick now, here, now, always ..."[60] Likewise "the children in the apple tree" are integral to the epiphany which concludes his Fourth Quartet 'Little Gidding' (1942).[61] In the Old Testament, enrichment and enlargement are God's promises to Zechariah for the restoration of Jerusalem if the people will only change. It will become a just, fulfilled and healthy society for old and young to enjoy, where: "the streets of the city shall be full of boys and girls playing in the streets thereof".[62]

Neilson was writing at a time when a tradition of sentimentalising childhood had become the Cult of the Child. It was discussed and celebrated in literature, theatre, art, dance and photography, attracting many writers and poets.[63] Novel, artificial, it was a counterbalance to

---

59 'The People in the Playground' (MR571).
60 T.S. Eliot, *Four Quartets,* Faber, London, 1945.
61 "It would not be fair to me to try and judge the new free verse. Very little of it has been read to me. Some of it by the Englishman Eliot, seems to contain passages of great beauty ... Many of our younger men may be able to express themselves better in this way than in rhyme." Neilson–J. Devaney, 9.iii.1941 and quoted in Devaney, *Shaw Neilson*, p. 188.
62 Zechariah 8:5.
63 See also Noel Macainsh, "John Shaw Neilson and the Cult of the Child", *Quadrant*, September, 1978, pp. 18–23.

the stark realities of the industrialisation of society, the crowded slums and the plight of child workers as depicted in Blake, Wordsworth and Dickens. Neilson's poems, often recalling imagery and rhythms from childhood games and songs, can be seen in this context. Like Blake, he created adult poetry out of the voice of children. Judith Wright recognised "such a voice, so morning-clear / as in your nursery tunes I hear".[64]

"Sweet lovers love the Spring" and, like Shakespeare, Neilson celebrates all the joy and new life the season brings. Spring "is the green love" and the 'Green Singer' (2). "For green indeed is a dear colour: / we learn to lisp thereon,[65] / Till we grow too tall for our first fair love / and the glories all are gone" ('Petticoat Green' [4]). His whimsical yarn 'Green Lover' (118draws on an old nursery rhyme about a frog and a lily-white duck.

The ring games of yore and Thomas Nashe's "maids dancing in a ring" are alluded to by Neilson in lines like: " 'Twas in a time when Love ran out and in", or "green joy running out and in", and "love like a sun ray ran out and in".[66] A ring-game, first collected by James Halliwell in 1842, with a variant described by the collector Alice B. Gomme in *The Traditional Games of England, Scotland, Ireland* (1894), was recalled as having been played in Western Victoria at the turn of the century, and quoted in the *Bulletin*, 19 March 1898. It was a reader's response to an article on children's songs and action games by Victor Daley. The words may have been familiar to Neilson.

---

64   Judith Wright, 'For John Shaw Neilson', *Judith Wright: Collected Poems*, Angus & Robertson, Sydney, Modern Poets, 1975 (1971), p. 237.
65   Note from Robert Burns 'Cotter's Saturday Night': "the lisping infant prattling on his knee."
66   From 'My Love Is Like a Violin' (MR412), 'The Little Girl with Black Hair' (MR390) and 'For a Child' (87).

> Green gravel, green gravel, the grass is so green
> The fairest young lady that ever was seen,
> We washed her in milk and we dressed her in silk,
> And we wrote down her name with a gold pen and ink.
> O Mary, O Mary your true love is dead,
> He's sent you a letter to turn round your head.[67]

Neilson responded strongly to rhythm and movement and he complimented Gilmore on one of her poems. " 'Little Dancer' I read often. I'm very fond of seeing kiddies dance."[68] "Dancing is a form of poetry," he told her, after witnessing a performance by Adeline Genée and Halina Schmolz with the Imperial Russian Ballet in Melbourne in 1913.[69]

An early poem, 'Which Colour?' is a like a chant from a children's game, "Which colour do you love best? / Which of the colours above the rest?" / I know not how to choose." Over many verses Neilson extends his chromatic scale: "I dearly love the green . . . red . . . blue, and white, the colour of angels' robes."[70] The poet was "assailed by colours". His world was a "tempest of all colour" filled with "green girls", "white eyelids", "blue winds", "white speech", "violet flutes", "red miles", "yellow air", "green petticoats", "the golden time", "red lovers", "the black season" and "moods of unmeasured magenta".

The "country versus city" is a theme which Neilson tackles in 'Out to the Green Fields' (117) and, as "a mild protest against hardness" and the commercialism of Melbourne, ugly in its grid-like conformity and "black with every sin" he wrote 'Stony Town' (122). "I think I have seen the expression 'I go as to a Fair' somewhere before. I am not sure. I suppose it will pass," he told Stephens.[71] Pass it does. Unlike Padraic

---

67 Ian Turner, *Cinderella Dressed in Yella*, Taplinger, Victoria, 1968, pp. 54–56, 124.
68 Neilson–M.Gilmore, 9.x.1919 (ML MSS A3267 V.16 PDMG); HH85.
69 Neilson–M. Gilmore, 11.i.1919 (ML MSS A3267: V.16 PDMCG); HH76–77. Halina Schmolz danced in the Australian premiere of Fokine's *The Dying Swan*.
70 'Which Colour' (MR279–81).

Colum's lament 'She Moved Through the Fair', 'Stony Town' is rhythmically boisterous, full of movement, and the imagery delights. When the Bush in its pastoral innocence comes to the City during the 1920s with skirts "a full thirty inches high", 'Stony Town' is overwhelmed by bells and laughter, the scent of lovers and cinnamon dust and the crowning glory of "the girl with a heat-wave in her hair". The poem has a rhythm redolent of an old milk-churning song that travelled the world.

> I was going to Kentucky,
> I was going to the Fair,
> I met a signorina with fandangles in her hair,
> Oh shake 'em, shake 'em, shake 'em, shake 'em if you can,
> If you cannot shake 'em,
> Do the best you can . . ." [72]

This is an adaptation of a rhyme still sung by Scots children today— "I was going to the country I was going to the fair I met a senorita with a curl in her hair . . ."[73]

Neilson describes his emotional response to reading Francis Thompson's poem 'Daisy' in a letter to Mary Gilmore.[74] "The last few stanzas brought tears to my eyes or almost so. Two lines are all I remember. 'The rose's scent is bitterness / To him that loved the rose.'" 'Daisy' is from *Poems on Childhood* (1893), and in it Thompson describes a tender moment between two children, a boy and girl picking wild raspberries together, before she goes artlessly on "her unremembering way". The poet looks back: "Still, still I seemed to see her, still /

---

71   Neilson–A.G. Stephens, 22.viii.1927 (ML MSS4937/5: 219–23 AGSP).
72   The Kentucky Fair was first held in 1816 and the early settlers localised this lively milk-churning rhyme. Another variant has "flowers in her hair". Today, children shake like a milkshake.
73   Ewan McVicar, *Doh Ray Me, When Ah Wis Wee*, Scots children's songs and rhymes, Berlinn Ltd, Edinburgh, 2007, p. 70.
74   Neilson–M. Gilmore, 26.iii.1914 (ML A3267 V.16 PDMG); HH59.

Look up with soft replies / And take the berries with her hand, / And the love with her lovely eyes." It is easy to see why Neilson should have been so moved. There is a clear link here to the lovelorn poet "a singer of the cold" in 'For a Little Girl's Birthday' (94) and again, in 'To a Schoolgirl' (98), who is addressed as "O most unconscious daisy!" The ageing poet wonders, "Can I, walled in by Autumn, / With buoyant things agree? / Speak all my heart to a daisy / If one should smile at me?"[75]

In an essay on the poet Shelley, Francis Thompson's outpourings over the prevailing Victorian attitude to childhood sadly are relevant today.[76]

> We of this self-conscious, incredulous generation, sentimentalise our children, analyse our children, think we are endowed with a special capacity to sympathise and identify ourselves with children; we play at being children. And the result is that we are not more child-like, but our children are less child-like ... Know you what it is to be a child? It is to be something very different from the man of today ... it is to believe in love, to believe in loveliness, to believe in belief; it is to be so little that the elves can reach to whisper in your ear ... it is to turn pumpkins into coaches and mice into horses, lowness into loftiness, and nothing into everything, for each child has its fairy godmother in its own soul; it is ... "To see a world in a grain of sand, / And a heaven in a wildflower, / Hold infinity in the palm of your hand, / And eternity in an hour."[77]

Thompson, Blake and Neilson all share a concern for the innocent child's right to a childhood. The "tawdry treacherous city", so attractive to the young, is an underworld. 'In the Street' (53) Neilson describes

---

75 Stephens sent Louise Dyer the original holograph of this poem with his purple annotation. "Written 1916. To Louise Dyer with the publs. compl. Good wishes 1923."
76 *The Works of Francis Thompson*, Vol. III, *Prose*, Burns Oats & Ashbourne Ltd, London, 1913, pp. 7–8.
77 William Blake, 'Auguries of Innocence', published London, 1863.

"the sly-eyed girls, the jeering boys" and 'In the Dim Counties' (107) he alludes to "little street wenches, / the callous, unclean". 'The Child Being There' (143), 'The Child we Lost' (66) and 'In the Street' (53) are poignant laments for lost innocence and Neilson expresses anxiety for a 'Little White Girl' (52), "the one thing white and clean . . . and pretty". Neilson tends to transform white dresses to shrouds and angels' robes, an idiosyncrasy suggesting he was more ready, certainly in the earlier years of writing, to accept and embrace the death of children than to tackle the often painful transition from childhood to maturity.

Neilson's recollection of a two-year-old girl asleep on a crowded train also provided inspiration. "I will try and put it in a rhyme some day", he told Gilmore. "Sleeping kiddies seem to appeal to us in a strange compelling manner do they not. Perhaps I'm a bit womanish in that way."[78] In 'Show Me the Song' (109) he declares: "Love will be loud as the sunlight, quiet as the moon, / Sweet as the sigh of a little child that shall waken soon."

"I am starting to write a Ballad, the longest I have attempted", he confided to Gilmore in 1919. "The central idea is Child Worship. Now I know you are interested."[79] Could this be the germ of an idea, which ultimately blossomed into 'The Orange Tree'? A young girl's awakening is interrupted by the persistent and hopeful questioning of the world-weary poet longing for "all happenings of the olden time".

> The young girl stood beside me. I
>   Saw not what her young eyes could see:
> —A light, she said, not of the sky
>   Lives somewhere in the Orange Tree.

---

78 Neilson–M. Gilmore, 13.ii.1921 (ML MSS A3267 V.16 PDMG); HH92.
79 Neilson–M. Gilmore, 30.xi.1919 (ML MSS123: 201 (a)-201 PDMG); HH88.

> —Is it, I said, of east or west?
>   The heartbeat of a luminous boy
> Who with his faltering flute confessed
>   Only the edges of his joy?
>
> Was he, I said, borne to the blue
>   In a mad escapade of Spring
> Ere he could make a fond adieu
>   To his love in the blossoming?

Mary Gilmore regarded 'The Orange Tree' as "the most supernatural poem in English, and the more so because there is nothing of the horrible in it, and nothing (on the other hand) of the saint's exaltation".[80] We know Neilson was partly inspired by Sandro Botticelli's *Primavera* and the orange groves where he picked fruit,[81] but it may be feasible given the date of his letter to Gilmore (1919) and Neilson's reference in a letter to James Devaney dated 28 October 1934, in which he was trying to recall when he had written some of his poems.

> I don't remember doing much writing in '14 or '15. 'Schoolgirl Hastening' must have been done about 1920. 'The Orange Tree' was finished the year before that [during 1919]. It started out of an old piece that I had discarded. I was trying to describe the people who visit St Kilda at the week-end holiday-making. I failed very badly. When I was working up in Merbein I could not help noticing the very beautiful light on the trees in the afternoon. I used the metre I had used in the St Kilda piece. I may have used one or two of the same lines. The other piece was a complete frost. I couldn't get going

---

80 M. Gilmore–Neilson, 24.i.1928 (ML MSS123, PDMG); HH184.
81 Sandro Botticelli (1445–1510), *Primavera* (tempera on panel) c.1478, Florence: Uffizi Gallery; James Devaney, *Shaw Neilson*, p.110. See HH428–29 for an analysis of the painting.

on it but the new beauty in the light on the oranges seemed to give me a lift.

'The Orange Tree' was not published in the *Bookfellow* until 15 February 1921, so Neilson's memory may not be entirely accurate.

Neilson was unnerved and brought to tears[82] reading the chapter 'The Golden Gates Are Passed' from George Eliot's *The Mill on the Floss*. It is the account of when the dark-haired, rebellious Maggie and her brother Tom go forth "into their new life of sorrow, and would never more see the sunshine undimmed by remembered cares".[83] The chapter title becomes a line in 'Maggie Tulliver' (26) and he goes on to quote Eliot's phrase 'Unseen Pity' in the final stanza. The childhood games, once shared by Neilson with his own sister, Maggie, and played by Maggie Tulliver with her fair-haired cousin Lucy, are described in 'The Land Where I Was Born' (8).

> Have you ever been down to my countree?
>   it was full of smiling queens:
> They had flaxen hair, they were white and fair,
>   but they never reached their teens.
> Their shoes were small and their dreams were tall:
>   wonderful frocks were worn;
> But the queens all strayed from the place we played
>   in the land where I was born.[84]

Another dark-haired girl was Florence Case, "a letter carrier" from Sea Lake. Neilson had known the family well and seen Florence grow from childhood into a young woman. She inspired Neilson's flirtatious tribute 'To Susette'[85] and 'Her Eyes' (43). The thirty-nine-year-old bachelor

---

82 Neilson–M. Gilmore, 20.x.1912 (ML MSS 123:155–163 PDMG); HH58.
83 George Eliot, *The Mill on the Floss*, A.S. Byatt (Ed.), Penguin Classics Edition, London, 1985 (1860).
84 Ibid. p. 117.

gave her a copy of *The Mill on The Floss*, inscribed in his own hand: "F. Case, Sea Lake, 7/7/11". In Irene Roche's memoir of the Case Family there is a brief reference:

> Mother told us that John Shaw Neilson had been in love with her, but that she did not think of him in a romantic way at all. No doubt she felt later in life that she must have hurt him in her younger days . . . "you can be rather cruel when you are young". She really thought of him as a dear family friend . . . [86]

By 1913 Florence had left the Post Office to work in Melbourne and was married a year later. Neilson's play on words in 'May' (25) composed in 1909 may refer to their friendship. "And undelivered lovers, half awake, / Hear noises in the dew."

There can only be speculation about Neilson's love for a woman in the so-called 'Sadie' poems, which range from sweet tenderness to passionate rage and inconsolable grief. They are from a period in his life he tried to conceal but the experience of loving and longing, pity and consolation continued to inspire his poetry.[87]

"I like the Spring Song, the white dresses, the sense of unworldliness",[88] he confessed to Gilmore. He blamed the neglect of his writing on "old age coming on . . . white dresses & pretty faces & beautiful weather in September and when the first frost comes, all these agitate me".[89] In 'Old Nell Dickerson' (14) he recounts the seasons:

---

85   'To Susette' (MR660).
86   Irene Roche, 'The Case Family and John Shaw Neilson', unpublished memoir, 1994 (HH). The copy of *The Mill on the Floss* contains newscuttings about Neilson and an added inscription "A gift to F. Case from John Shaw Neilson Australian Poet". Florence Case attended Neilson's funeral held on 14 May 1942 at Footscray Cemetery.
87   See also Cliff Hanna, 'Shaw Neilson's "1912" Notebook: A Diary of Lost Love', *Meridian*, Vol. 9. No. 2, October 1990, pp. 111–21.
88   Neilson–M. Gilmore, 31.xii.1916 (ML MSS123: 375–77, PDMG); HH68.
89   Neilson–M. Gilmore, 20.i.1918 (ML MSS 123: 11–14, PDMG); HH73.

> The summer sauntered in with wheat
> and forest fire and haze,
> And the white frocks of white girls,
> and lads with love ablaze . . .

White dresses recall James McNeill Whistler, *Symphony in White No. 1* (1862), portraits by Tom Roberts, Charles Conder's *plein air* canvas *Springtime* (1888) and fashion plates and photography from the *Lone Hand*. Neilson's inspiration for 'Oh Player of the Flute', "let us together / Enter the charmed towns of intense wine / Where the white girls whiten the white weather" came from reading about "Venetian painters who could paint a white cloud on a white sky".[90]

Drawing on traditional motifs, as did the Scottish poet Allan Cunningham, when he extolled a sixteen-year-old as a "honey pear" and a seventeen-year-old as "drop-ripe",[91] Neilson reported to Stephens in 1923: "I am again trying a girl, say about 16, a momentous creature. I may get something ready for August or Sept."[92] The age of seventeen represents a turning point, the leaving behind of adolescence, and it is sensitively exploited by Neilson in 'The Flight of the Weary' (139) and 'The Child We Lost' (66)—"the seasons sixteen times had turned". These ballads are sentimental in the late-nineteenth-century manner, recalling narratives of Robert Buchanan, such as 'Euphrosyne'. "A little maid of seventeen Mays, / A happy child with golden hair. / What should she know of Love's wild ways, / Its hopes, its pain, and prayer?"[93]

From the eighteenth century onwards many of the more robust ballads shocked editors into 'a frenzy of emendation', although there re-

---

90   Neilson–A.G. Stephens, 5.i.1916 (ML MSS4937/4:505–06 AGSP), (MR422–24); HH65.
91   'My Lassie Wi' the Sunny Locks', *Poems and Songs by Allan Cunningham 1784–1842*, John Murray, London, 1847.
92   Neilson–A.G. Stephens, 6.vii.1923 (ML MSS4937/8 AGSP); HH109.
93   R.W. Buchanan, *The Complete Poetical Works*, Chatto & Windus, London, 1884 (1901 reprint).

mains a version of 'I'm Seventeen Come Sunday'[94] rewritten in 1792 by Cunningham's young friend, Robert Burns.[95] Typically it is about temptation, declaration and seduction, but the young girl is not "undone for ever". As a soldier's wife "the drum and fife is her delight, / And a merry man in the morning." In this context "a merry man" is willing and amorously inclined and no doubt this is behind Neilson's injunction: "Let us be making merry: / Lovers at middle moon / With their kissing have taught us . . ."[96]

Robert Herrick's 'Delight in Disorder' reprinted in Palgrave's has been noted previously to record Julia's 'tempestuous petticote', and here is another motif Neilson plays with. Of particular interest is Donald Low's discovery of Robert Burns' additional lines for 'Coming Through the Rye'.

> Coming through the rye,
> She draiglet a' her petticoatie,
> Coming through the rye.
> Jenny's a' wat, poor body;
> Jenny's seldom dry;
> She draiglet a' her petticoatie,
> Coming through the rye.[97]

---

94 Collected by George Butterworth & R.O. Morris, W.G. Whittaker (Gen. Ed.), Oxford University Press. While a guest of Louise Dyer in Melbourne, Dr Whittaker composed a number of settings for Neilson's poems which were sung by Evelyn Scotney at the Albert Hall in London during the late 1920s.
95 James Reeves, *The Idiom of the People*, 1958. Reeves re-examined Cecil Sharp's manuscript and restored many of the lyrics to their unexpurgated form.
96 'Let Us Be Making Merry' (MR382).
97 Rye: river, draiglet: drenched. In Thomas Mansfield's manuscript (1770–80) at Broughton House, Kircudbright. Discovered by Donald A. Low (Ed.), *The Songs of Robert Burns*, Routledge, London, 1993, cited in *Studies in Scottish Literature*, Vol. I, July 1963, p. 56.

Neilson is both tender and witty in 'In The Wind',[98] an unpublished, earlier version of 'The Petticoat Plays' (56). Here he puns on the word 'wed' with its old Scottish meaning 'to pledge'. "May she have love asleep, / She wed not any sigh. / This is her petticoat / The wind will dry." The discarded stanza from the first draft of 'The Petticoat Plays'[99]—"Speak to me little wind / Softly oh sky / Faintly her petticoat / Sings and is dry". Fortunately we have—uncensored—Neilson's delicate conclusion to 'The Eleventh Moon' (96). "The moon did seem as music spilled upon her spotless gown, / And at her height of happiness the summer tear came down. / Night—and the silence honey-wet—the moon came to the full: / It was a time for gentle thought and the gathering of wool." Stephens was curious. Was Neilson becoming "too mystical and cloudy... Is there a slang use of 'wool gathering'—or is it your own? You see what it implies—not that I mind."[100]

Strains of Irish folklore and ballad inevitably make themselves felt in Neilson's work. The white petticoat worn by a young girl of seventeen, "almost a woman—half-awake" symbolised virginity.[101] The young girl preparing for courtship in the 'Three Lovely Lasses' sings, "I'm sending my shoes to be mended / And my petticoat to be dyed green".

Dyed red attested to marriage. 'Siúil a Rúin' ('Come O Love') is based on a traditional Irish lament for a lover who has broken his promise and gone to fight in France. The girl sings "I'll dye my petticoats, / I'll dye them red / And round the world I'll beg my bread / Until my parents shall wish me dead..."[102]

A child conceived out of wedlock caused shame and often suicide or infanticide followed. As themes in Neilson's poetry,[103] they are fore-

---

98   'In The Wind' (MR363–64).
99   'The Petticoat Plays' (MR573).
100 A.G. Stephens–Neilson, 8.ii.1920 (NLA MS 1145/30 HFCC); HH90.
101 'To Dulcie in a White Dress' (MR1150).
102 William Cole (Ed.), *Folk Songs of England, Ireland, Scotland and Wales*, Warner Bros Publications Inc., Miami, 1961, pp. 64–67.
103 'Child of Tears' (55). 'Marian's Child' (MR129) draws on George Eliot's *Adam Bede* (1859).

shadowed in Padraic Colum's 'The Young Girl' (after the Irish), who gave herself and offered a dowry but her lover has "kept far away". If he does not return "The petticoat in the dye-pot here / Will never fast its red" and "her dress will be the sheet bleached there, / My place, below the clay".[104]

For Neilson the petticoat "is a tender thing, tender as love and dew" and is to be painted in a synaesthetic blending of sound, colour and movement. An artist, full of ideas for 'Petticoat Green' (4), he writes to Stephens:

> In it I am asking a melancholy painter to paint me an ordinary petticoat or underskirt green because green I take to be the colour of youth and all joy. The Petticoat in this too represents for me Woman at her most charming time 16 to 20. The petticoat will be merely used by the painter to express everything in his heart and eyes.
>
> 'Twill all come easily Love, Hate, Peace, War, Youth, Age, Play, Toil, Other Lands, Other Times, Witches, Fairies, Dairymaids, everything in the rhyme and everything I can't get in. I shall read as much or more than the artist can paint.[105]

Some years later Neilson was to remark that 'Petticoat Green' (4) and 'The Wedding in September' (78) were "twins in spirit". "They rumble about the influence of colour and sound on the human being."[106] Delighted that Nettie Palmer's children recited 'Petticoat Green', Neilson explained: "I was taking some medicine with morphia in it ... and I suppose the drug kept me flapping a bit longer than usual."[107] Louise Dyer dressed in green velvet to recite the poem at a Melbourne soirée. "One worthy gentleman whom I know," confided Neilson, "thought that

---

104 See also Peter Kuch, 'John Shaw Neilson and Padraic Colum', *Meridian*, Vol. 9, October 1990, pp. 122–32.
105 Neilson–A.G. Stephen, 5.i.1916 (ML MSS 4937/4:505–6 AGSP); HH64.
106 Neilson–J. Devaney, 28.x.1934 (NLA MS 1145/68 HFCC); HH277.
107 Neilson–Nettie Palmer, 7.vii.1921 (NLA MS 1174/1/2385); HH93–94.

I owed him an explanation of that Rhyme; that is what one meets with. I don't think people ought to ask such questions."[108]

Stephens and others linked Neilson's poetry with William Blake's subversively simple vision expressed in ballad, hymn and children's rhymes to lay bare the 'Two Contrary States of the Human Soul'. Understandably the suggestion he may have been influenced by Blake annoyed Neilson to the extent that he claimed in the year before his death that he had never read a line of Blake's poetry in his life![109] While poets can share a common matrix the art is in their individual creativity. Walter Murdoch, when reviewing the *Collected Poems*, wrote that although Neilson was not a lettered poet and was outside literary movements and metrical experiments, this was to his advantage.

> A great body of Australian verse had been bookish in inspiration and imitative . . . trying to do in a local setting what had been done elsewhere before. [Neilson's] big disadvantage has been in the restricting of his metrical patterns and . . . his field of language . . . but these are offset by his great gift for singing thought and for singing words and his considerable skill in weaving rhythm . . . He is a lyric poet . . . it is life seen with clear eyes You remember Coleridge: "the poet is one who carries the simplicity of childhood into the power of manhood; who with a soul unsubdued by habit, unshackled by custom, contemplates all things with the freshness of a child" . . . "Freshness" and wonder. It would be hard to find two better words for the way Shaw Neilson looks at the world . . . [110]

Neilson's poetry inspires. He is a symbolist, a mystic, and a seeker of beauty, love and pity. For him the dream is deep.

---

108   Neilson–L. Dyer, 20.ix.23 (LaT MS1070 LH-DP); HH110.
109   Brisbane *Telegraph*, 2 July 1941. Cited by C. Hanna, *The Folly of Spring*, University of Queensland Press, St Lucia, 1990, p. 5.
110   Polygon [Walter Murdoch], *West Australian*, 3 August 1935; HH417.

> The man God made he dreameth deep
> Down in his heart. High in the air
> His heaven lies. How shall he sleep?
> He had a dream—the dream was fair.

Acknowledgements

I am grateful to Dr Jenny Blain, Susan Bee and Alan Hewson for their suggestions and to Professor Robert Dixon for his encouragement with my research. I have benefited from access to material in the La Trobe Library, Victoria, the Mitchell Library, New South Wales and the National Library of Australia, Canberra and Margaret Robert's electronic Variorum Edition *John Shaw Neilson, The Collected Poems*, from the Australian Scholarly Editions Centre UNSW at ADFA, Canberra, 2003. I have been glad of the practical assistance received from Sydney University Press and the interest shown in my work over many years by the John Shaw Neilson Society.

Introduction

R.H. Croll

WHEN Australia makes up its account with the late A.G. Stephens, one of the outstanding items in its indebtedness to that able critic will obviously be his early and helpful recognition of the genius of John Shaw Neilson. In a world so given to what it calls the practical, courage is needed to back an unknown writer. "A.G.S." had that courage. It was he who produced Neilson's three books and he was bold enough, in very early days, to acclaim John Shaw Neilson as "first of Australian poets."

Many good judges have followed Stephens. "This delicate singer should be proclaimed as part of our heritage," wrote Nettie Palmer; Frank Wilmot ("Furnley Maurice") declared that "a writer like Neilson stands high and alone among the Australians"; Mary Gilmore also placed him above everyone here—"I class him with Blake and Keats", was her verdict.

It was in 1919 that his first book, *Heart of Spring*, appeared, and in 1923 came *Ballad and Lyrical Poems*, this second collection repeating many of the poems published in its predecessor. Here gratefully must be acknowledged the kindness of Mrs Louise Dyer, then of Melbourne, now residing in Paris, but for whose generosity the *Ballad and Lyrical Poems* volume would possibly not have appeared. Both of these works are now out of print, and copies of his third book, *New Poems* (1927) are difficult to procure.

So assured is John Shaw Neilson's place in Australian letters that the inability to obtain his work constitutes a definite loss to students of the subject and to lovers of the best in our literature. The time has arrived:

this collected edition is put out to meet the need that so patently exists. It contains all that the poet himself considers worth preserving of his three earlier volumes, together with certain fresh poems hitherto uncollected.

John Shaw Neilson was born at Penola, South Australia, on the 22nd February, 1872. His grandparents were William Neilson and Jessie MacFarlane of Cupar, and, on his mother's side, Neil McKinnon of Skye, and Margaret Stuart of Greenock. His father, John Neilson, was a farmer and contractor who removed to Victoria when the boy, John Shaw, was nine years of age.

The lad was destined to follow the life of the ordinary bush-worker. Only of recent years has he known other than hard manual labour as a means of living. It is an amazing thing that his mind could retain its refinement unsullied and breed loveliness amidst the rough surroundings of his daily tasks.

He was given little schooling, but he had the singing blood and the singing heart and a native impulse towards culture which has enabled him to surmount all difficulties of expression. He is true poet; moreover he is a skilled artist in complete command of the means of stating his thoughts. Anything unusual in form is deliberate and commonly chosen with insight and skill.

In attempting to trace the sources of his decided gift it must be remembered that the father had also some of the genuine poetic fire. Here are the two concluding verses of an effort by his father, titled "The Last Time".

> The goodly ships lie broken at the haven,
> Fair tresses float upon the heaving tide;
> And riderless the steed comes home at even:
> The unseen shadow follows by our side,
> Follows through winter's chill and summer's prime
> Until we say Good-bye "For the last time."

> But we shall meet again, love cannot die;
> In life infinite soul with soul shall blend
> In other worlds, be the time far or nigh:
> Surely this little life is not the end:
> And tears will fall in heavenly spheres sublime
> And sighing sorrow weep "For the last time."

Mysteries John Shaw Neilson may have, and has, as in the fascinating set of verses he has named 'The Orange Tree', but who would deny a poet the privilege of reserves beyond reach of the general? Customarily his meaning is clear, his diction simple and expressive. "Let your song be delicate", he wrote, and never was word better chosen to describe his own utterances.
Beautiful thoughts and beautiful lines are showered on us—

> Let your voice be delicate,
> The bees are home,
> All their day's love is sunken
> Safe in the comb. ['Song be Delicate']

> Shyly the silver-hatted mushrooms make
> Soft entrance through . . .
> Faint as a widow mourning with soft eyes . . . ['May']

> Softly as griefs call
> In a violin . . . ['Love's Coming']

It has been truly said of Neilson's work that it has the dew on it.

Melbourne, March 1934

To
Louise Dyer
In gratitude

Collected Poems of John Shaw Neilson

Heart of Spring!

    O HEART of Spring!
Spirit of light and love and joyous day
So soon to faint beneath the fiery Summer:
Still smiles the Earth, eager for thee alway:
Welcome art thou, so ever short thy stay,
Thou bold, thou blithe newcomer!
Whither, oh whither this thy journeying,
    O Heart of Spring!

    O Heart of Spring!
After the stormy days of Winter's reign
When the keen winds their last lament are sighing
The Sun shall raise thee up to life again:
In thy dim death thou shalt not suffer pain:
Surely thou dost not fear this quiet dying?
Whither, oh whither blithely journeying,
    O Heart of Spring!

    O Heart of Spring!
Youth's emblem, ancient as unchanging light,
Uncomprehended, unconsumed, still burning:
Oh that we could, as thee, rise from the night
To find a world of blossoms lilac-white
And long-winged swallows unafraid returning . . .
Whither, oh whither this thy journeying,
    O Heart of Spring!

Green Singer

ALL singers have shadows
    that follow like fears,
But I know a singer
    who never saw tears:
A gay love—a green love—
    delightsome! divine!
The Spring is that singer—
    an old love of mine!

All players have shadows
    and into the play
Old sorrows will saunter—
    old sorrows will stay.
But here is a player
    whose speech is divine!
The Spring is that player—
    an old love of mine!

All singers grow heavy:
    the hours as they run
Bite up all the blossoms,
    suck up all the sun.
But I know a singer,
    delightsome! divine!
The gay love—the green love—
    an old love of mine!

Song Be Delicate

LET your song be delicate.
    The skies declare
No war—the eyes of lovers
    Wake everywhere.

Let your voice be delicate.
    How faint a thing
Is Love, little Love crying
    Under the Spring.

Let your song be delicate.
    The flowers can hear:
Too well they know the tremble,
    Of the hollow year.

Let your voice be delicate.
    The bees are home:
All their day's love is sunken
    Safe in the comb.

Let your song be delicate.
    Sing no loud hymn:
Death is abroad . . . oh, the black season!
    The deep—the dim!

Petticoat Green

I WOULD not ask of a joyful man
    for his heart would be too cold;
And I would go on a long journey
    to a country ripe and old:
I would like to walk where the mad folk went
    and never a soul was mean;
—'Twill all come easily, mournful man!
    if you paint me a petticoat green.

Oh, every feud is a lifelong feud
    and every fight is fair:
The girls have eyes and the men have blood
    and the swords are sharp and bare:
The witches fight with the dairymaids
    and the fairies still are seen:
—'Twill all come easily, mournful man!
    if you paint me a petticoat green.

For green indeed is a dear colour:
    we learn to lisp thereon,
Till we grow too tall for our first fair love
    and the glories all are gone;
And when at length we have footed it well
    our eyes grow tender then:
We sit and talk when we may not walk,
    we are close to the green again.

A petticoat is a tender thing,
    tender as love or dew,
Perhaps it is piece of an angel's garb
    that has sometime fallen through;
For there be gates in the distant sky
    that the elder seers have seen,
And you—you have known them, mournful man!
    so paint me a petticoat green.

Paint me all that the children laugh
    in a long white afternoon:
Paint me all that the old men know
    when they croak to the setting moon:
Paint me flowers and the death of flowers
    and the tenderlings that grew
Between the time of the north wind
    and the kindness of the dew.

Paint me eyes on a holiday
    and the long kiss of a bride:
Paint me ashes and dying men
    And the shriek when a woman died:
Mournful man, there is love in you
    but your big tears come between:
Grant me a favour, mournful man!
    and paint me a petticoat green.

Paint me joy in a whistling dance
   and gloom on a heavy hill:
Paint me reeds and a water-bird
   and a matchless maiden's will:
Paint me men who have laughed at death
   and hope that is good to see:
—I know you have known it, mournful man!
   you can beckon it up to me.

Paint me prisons of olden times
   and the flight of the butterflies:
Paint me all that the madmen see
   when they speak to the sullen skies:
Paint me rogues that are loth to die
   and the sighing of honest men:
Paint me Youth that is weak and worn
   and Age that is young again.

I would not ask of a joyful man
   for his heart would be too cold;
But the love is deep in you, mournful man!
   though your speech is white and old:
Paint me lilies and summer maids
   and skeletons—all are clean—
'Twill all come easily, mournful man!
   if you paint me a petticoat green.

Greeting

FILL up! fill up! to-day we meet:
    What of the wind? Who knows the weather?
Shall we be old men in the street?
    (Fill up! fill up!—to-day we meet!)
We, who have found the eager feet
    That kindly God is loth to tether.
Fill up! fill up! to-day we meet!
    What of the wind? Who knows the weather?

The Land Where I Was Born

HAVE you ever been down to my countree
    where the trees are green and tall?
The days are long and the heavens are high,
    but the people there are small.
There is no work there: it is always play:
    the sun is sweet in the morn;
But a thousand dark things walk at night
    in the land where I was born.

Have you ever been down to my countree
    where the birds made happy Spring?
The parrots screamed from the honey-trees
    and the jays hopped chattering.
Strange were the ways of the water-birds
    in the brown swamps, night and morn:
I knew the roads they had in the reeds
    in the land where I was born.

Have you ever been down to my countree
    have you ridden the horses there?
They had silver manes, and we made them prance,
    and plunge and gallop and rear.
We were knights of the olden time
    when the old chain-mail was worn:
The swords would flash! and the helmets crash!
    in the land where I was born.

Have you ever been down to my countree?
    it was full of smiling queens:
They had flaxen hair, they were white and fair,
    but they never reached their teens.
Their shoes were small and their dreams were tall:
    wonderful frocks were worn;
But the queens all strayed from the place we played
    in the land where I was born.

I know you have been to my countree
    though I never saw you there;
I know you have loved all things I loved,
    flowery and sweet and fair.
The days were long—it was always play;
    but we,—we are tired and worn:
They could not welcome us back again
    to the land where I was born.

The Sun Is Up

SPEAK not of Death: it is a merry morn;
A glittering bird has danced into a tree:
From his abundant heart bravely are borne
The loves of leafy choristers to me:
Music is of the sunlight, strong and free . . .
The sun is up, and Death is far away:
The first hour is the sweetest of the day.

Blithely a bush boy wanders on a walk—
Shaking with joy, joyous in heart and limb:
For his delight the trees have learned to talk
And all the flowers have little laughs with him
Watching the far sky, wonderful and dim . . .
The sun is up, and Death is far away:
The first hour is the sweetest of the day.

Pale Neighbour

OVER the road she lives not far,
   My neighbour pale and thin:
"Sweet is the world!" she cries, "how sweet
   To keep on living in!"

Her heart it is a right red heart
   That cannot stoop to pine;
Her hand-clasp is a happiness,
   Her welcome is a wine.

Love, she will have it, is a lilt
   From some lost comedy
Played long ago when the white stars
   Lightened the greenery.

Ever she talks of earth and air
   and sunlit junketing:
Gaily she says, "I know I shall
   Be dancing in the Spring!"

Almost I fear her low, low voice
   As one may fear the moon,
As one may fear too faint a sound
   In an old uncanny tune.

. . . Over the road 'twill not be long—
    Clearly I see it all . . .
Ere ever the red days come up
    Or the pale grasses fall.

There will be black upon us, and
    Within our eyes a dew:
We shall be walking neighbourly
    As neighbours—two and two.

To a Blue Flower

I WOULD be dismal with all the fine pearls of
   the crown of a king;
But I can talk plainly to you, you little blue
   flower of the Spring!

Here in the heart of September the world that
   I walk in is full
Of the hot happy sound of the shearing, the rude
   heavy scent of the wool.

Soon would I tire of all riches or honours or
   power that they fling;
But you are my own, of my own folk, you little
   blue flower of the Spring!

I was around by the cherries to-day; all the
   cherries are pale:
The world is a woman in velvet: the air is the
   colour of ale.

I would be dismal with all the fine pearls of the
   crown of a king;
But I can give love-talk to you, you little blue
   flower of the Spring!

Old Nell Dickerson

THE young folk heard the old folk say
    'twas long ago she came;
Some said it was her own, and some it
    was another's shame.
All pleasantly the seasons passed
    in gray and gold and green,
But the heart of old Nell Dickerson
    no one had ever seen.

They said that when a baby crowed
    she turned her head away,
And when delightful lovers kissed
    her sallow face went gray:
Some say she laughed at love and death
    and every man-made law—
But the heart of old Nell Dickerson
    no babbler ever saw.

October ran with greenery
    and blossoms white and fair;
The poorest soul had time to feast
    on beauty everywhere;
A thousand anthems rose to God
    through the uproarious blue,
But the heart of old Nell Dickerson
    no singer ever knew.

The summer sauntered in with wheat
    and forest fire and haze,
And the white frocks of white girls,
    and lads with love ablaze;
Sweet sighs were in the high heavens
    and upon the warm ground—
But the heart of old Nell Dickerson
    it never yet was found.

The winter came with wistful
    talk of water-birds in tune,
And while their snowy treasures slept
    did mother ewes commune;
In every wind and every rain
    some daring joys would climb—
But the heart of old Nell Dickerson
    was prisoner all the time.

The streamers stood across the sky
    one evening clear and warm;
The old folk said the streamers come
    foretelling strife and storm.
When old Nell laughed her hollow laugh
    the neighbours looked in awe,
But the heart of old Nell Dickerson
    no neighbour ever saw.

And with the night came thundering
    like Evil wandering near,
And the tender little children wept
    and the women shook with fear;
Out on the night went one stern soul—
    along the wind it blew;
Oh, the heart of old Nell Dickerson
    no babbler ever knew!

Softly they sought her little room,
    and she was blue and cold;
Upon the wall some straggling words
    her last poor wishes told:
Nothing she gave, and little begged—
    they read there mournfully:
"Bitter and black was all my life,
    but wear no black for me."

* * * * *

'Twas a green day and a wild day
   and lovers walked along,
And the old men, the grey men,
   the ruddy men and strong,
And the tenderest of pale girls
   in pink and green and blue
Walked mournfully behind the heart
   that no one ever knew.

And there were many dropping tears
   on sashes red and wide,
And more hot prayers were said that day
   than if a king had died;
And some wore white and yellow frocks
   and some wore blue and green,
But the heart of old Nell Dickerson
   no one had ever seen.

Along a River

GREEN leaves—a patch of world along a river,
    The drab and silver draping every limb,
The cackling kingfisher with throat a-quiver
    Eager to sing for us a morning hymn.

By yonder trees the rough red rock hangs over
    The black duck's brood—a little fleet at sea;
In the far sky a wicked foe doth hover:
    A plover calls—it is a call for me.

Across the stream, slowly and with much shrinking
    Softly a full-eyed wallaby descends
To the blue water's edge . . . I see him drinking . . .
    And he and I and all his folk are friends.

Julie Callaway

THIS world, I always call it mine,
    Because no other world I know:
Love it or hate it, how you will,
    With kindness like the overflow
Of some bare river rambling on,
    So does it only seek to bless:
—Oh, dry your tears! for, all things gone,
The old world kindly wanders on.

This world of mine, this world of yours:
    November, and a glorious day,
So drowsily the bees did hum
    And pretty Julie Callaway
Stood laughing, lingering at the door . . .
    Of all this sweetness, grace and gleam
The old-time singers sang of yore;
So let us all sing evermore.

The air grew sweeter; days were long;
    Yet everywhere beneath the sky
Death, who would never be gainsaid,
    Sat waiting with a watchful eye . . .
On every tree there comes a flower,
    To every lad and lass a time—
A dancing day, a month, an hour—
The gold world trembles in a shower.

Oh, pretty Julie Callaway,
    God surely loved her for her dream—
A little home not far away . . .
    How wonderful the world may seem
When one we love (and Love is strong)
    Walks with us in the flowery way:
All else that in the world is wrong,
How soon forgotten. Love is long.

It is not far, you see her grave,
    'Tis in the shadow of the trees;
I sometimes fancy Julie hears
    The mid-day murmuring of the bees
And knows our footsteps every way
    And this sweet world to her denied.
—'Twas in the bloom of bride's array
She died, upon her wedding day.

And is God merciful or kind?
    He knoweth all, full well He knew
Millions of hard, sin-maddened men
    And wasting, worn-out women too,
Praying for Death, as devils pray;
    And she pure-hearted, beautiful . . .
In orange bloom, in bride's array,
Death found her on her wedding day.

At a Lowan's Nest

HERE, in the rubble and the sand,
This monument by thee was planned:
Great was the love that in thee hid,
O, builder of the Pyramid!

By no delirious king compelled
But by the mother-heart upheld,
Little of pain or toil thou recked,
Brave builder! eager architect!

This and no other was thy shrine:
This monument to birth was thine:
Great was the love within thee hid,
O, builder of the Pyramid!

Old Granny Sullivan

A PLEASANT shady place it is, a pleasant place and cool—
The township folk go up and down, the children pass to school:
Along the river lies my world, a dear sweet world to me;
I sit and learn—I cannot go: there is so much to see.

But Granny she has seen the world, and often by her side
I sit and listen while she speaks of all that women pride.
Old Granny's hands are clasped; she wears her favourite faded shawl—
I ask her this, I ask her that: she says, "I mind them all".

The boys and girls that Granny knew, far o'er the seas are they;
But there's no love like the old love, and the old world far away.
Her talk is all of wakes and fairs—or how, when night would fall,
" 'Twas many a quare thing crept and came!" And Granny "minds them
      all".

A strange new land was this to her, and perilous, rude and wild—
Where loneliness and tears and care came to each mother's child:
The wilderness closed all around, grim as a prison wall;
But white folk then were stout of heart—Ah! Granny "minds it all".

The day she first met Sullivan—she tells it all to me—
How she was hardly twenty-one, and he was twenty-three.
The courting days! the kissing days!—but bitter things befall
The bravest hearts that plan and dream. Old Granny "minds it all".

Her wedding dress I know by heart: yes! every flounce and frill;
And the little home they lived in first, with the garden on the hill.
'Twas there her baby boy was born, and neighbours came to call;
But none had seen a boy like Jim—and Granny "minds it all".

They had their fight in those old days; but Sullivan was strong,
A smart quick man at anything; 'Twas hard to put him wrong . . .
One day they brought him from the mine . . . (The big salt tears will fall)
   . . .
" 'Twas long ago, God rest his soul!" Poor Granny "minds it all".

The first dark days of widowhood, the weary days and slow,
The grim, disheartening, uphill fight, then Granny lived to know.
"The childer," ah! they grew and grew—sound, rosy-cheeked, and tall:
"The childer" still they are to her. Old Granny "minds them all".

How well she loved her little brood! Oh, Granny's heart was brave!
She gave to them her love and faith—all that the good God gave.
They change not with the changing years: as babies just the same
She feels for them—though some, alas, have brought her grief and shame.

The big world called them here and there, and many a mile away:
They cannot come—she cannot go—the darkness haunts the day;
And I, no flesh and blood of hers, sit here while shadows fall—
I sit and listen-Granny talks; for Granny "minds it all".

'Tis time to pause, for pause we must—we only have our day
Yes; by and by our dance will die, our fiddlers cease to play:
And we shall seek some quiet place where great grey shadows fall,
And sit and wait as Granny waits-we'll sit and "mind them all".

May

SHYLY the silver-hatted mushrooms make
    Soft entrance through,
And undelivered lovers, half awake,
    Hear noises in the dew.

Yellow in all the earth and in the skies,
    The world would seem
Faint as a widow mourning with soft eyes
    And falling into dream.

Up the long hill I see the slow plough leave
    Furrows of brown;
Dim is the day and beautiful: I grieve
    To see the sun go down.

But there are suns a many for mine eyes
    Day after day:
Delightsome in grave greenery they rise,
    Red oranges in May.

Maggie Tulliver

I SEE the old-time mill, the old-time miller,
    The peaceful river in a pleasant land;
And you, the dark-eyed dear rebellious Maggie
    They could not understand.

Love in the bud . . . hedgerows and English meadows . . .
    The sunlight's flickering shadows gathering fast . . .
And your big tears because the world has gripped you,
    The golden gates are passed.

Dreamer of many dreams from the beginning!
    Eager to love, eager to spoil and spend!
Into your life God put a crooked lover
    And pity, love's old friend.

Anon I see a tall man proudly fashioned,
    A full, sweet woman, lovable and fair . . .
What of the path? Sweet flowers and sharp-edged perils
    And bleeding hearts are there.

The world has branded you a false, foul sinner:
    It is not merciful and you were rash . . .
Up at the whipping-post your white flesh trembled:
    You felt the cruel lash!

In the last anguish does the Unseen Pity
    See the long wrestlings of this flesh and blood?
—But Death was kind to you, dear dark-eyed Maggie
    Who walked into the flood.

Break of Day

THE stars are pale.
Old is the Night, his case is grievous,
    His strength doth fail.

Through stilly hours
The dews have draped with Love's old lavishness
    The drowsy flowers.

And Night shall die,
Already, lo! the Morn's first ecstasies
    Across the sky.

An evil time is done.
Again as some one lost in a quaint parable,
    Comes up the Sun.

Sheedy Was Dying

GREY as a rising ghost,
    Helpless and dumb;
This he had feared the most—
    Now it had come:
Through the tent door,
    Mocking, defying,
The Thirsty Land lay,
    —And Sheedy was dying!

Why should he ever
    Keep turning, keep turning
All his thoughts over
    To quicken their burning?
Why should the North wind speak.
    Creeping and crying?
—Who else could mourn for him?
Sheedy was dying!

Ay! he had travelled far—
    Homeless, a rover;
Drunk his good share and more
    Half the world over;
So now had ended
    All toiling and trying:
Out in his tent alone
    Sheedy was dying!

Never a priest to make
    Prayer to his travel
Out to that mist of things
    None may unravel.
Steering out, staring out,
    And the wind crying,
Who else could mourn for him,
    Sheedy was dying.

Kind, in a surly way;
    Somewhat rough-spoken;
Truth to his fellow-men
    Keeping unbroken;
A strong man, he stood without
    Flinching or sighing—
Now, on his bunk alone,
    Sheedy was dying!

Birds of the Thirsty Land
    In the dull grey . . .
Mist of the even-time
    Floating away . . .
Still did the North wind speak,
    Creeping and crying:
White, with his mouth agape,
    Sheedy was dying!

The Eyes of Little Charlotte

NOW God has made a wistful world
    And a woman strangely coy:
Her eyes say come, and go, and come,
    And stay and be a boy.
Oh, the eyes of little Charlotte say
    Come, kiss me if you can!
But in a trice they change and cry
    Go out and be a man.

Oh, the eyes of little Charlotte say
    You shall not flinch at pain;
You shall not sigh for the cool cities
    Or moan for the soft rain.
The wind shall bite you, throat and cheek;
    The sun shall leave its tan;
But the eyes of little Charlotte say
    Go out and be a man.

And you shall speak as a man speaks,
    Not mealy-mouthed or mild,
But you must go with a girl's love
    For every lisping child;
Nor shall you live in the far clouds
    As only dreamers can:
For the eyes of little Charlotte say
    Go out and be a man.

And you shall fight as a man fights
    And fare as a man may;
And you shall see as giants see
    And hear what giants say;
You shall not bide in a safe place
    Near by a lady's fan—
For the eyes of little Charlotte say
    Go out and be a man.

And your reward,—the old reward
    That is for all who dare,
The long love of a warm woman
    And kisses, proud and fair.
Oh, you shall toil for Love—the Law
    Since ever Love began—
For the eyes of little Charlotte say
    Go out and be a man.

Meeting of Sighs

YOUR voice was the rugged
   old voice that I knew;
I gave the best grip of
   my greeting to you.
I know not of your lips—
   you knew not of mine;
Of travel and travail
   we gave not a sign.

We drank and we chorused
   with quips in our eyes;
But under our song was
   the meeting of sighs.
I knew not of your lips—
   you knew not of mine;
For lean years and lone years
   had watered the wine.

Old Violin

SPEAK not to me, old violin!
    Mock not this heart of mine!
Thou mummy with the glistening skin
Speak not to me, old violin!
For the dead men have shadows thin,
    And all their sobs are thine—
Speak not to me, old violin!
    Mock not this heart of mine!!

Love's Coming

QUIETLY as rosebuds
   Talk to the thin air,
Love came so lightly
   I knew not he was there.

Quietly as lovers
   Creep at the middle moon,
Softly as players tremble
   In the tears of a tune;

Quietly as lilies
   Their faint vows declare
Came the shy pilgrim:
   I knew not he was there.

Quietly as tears fall
   On a wild sin,
Softly as griefs call
   In a violin;

Without hail or tempest,
   Blue sword or flame,
Love came so lightly
   I knew not that he came.

The Lover Sings

IT is not dark; it is not day;
    The earth lies quivering to the dew:
Shall we not love her? All men may.
    Lo, here a lover passes too!
Down a green shadowy path he goes
And in his hand he bears a rose,
    Still singing that his heart is true.

Creeps the low darkness where the eve
    Groweth more gloomy; and anon
The lover sings. And doth he grieve
    For red-lip kisses three days gone?
Hark how he sings! high heavenly clear,
Chief messenger of light to cheer
    The brown earth and that bides thereon.

Listen, and we shall leave the earth,
    Brooding no more o'er baser things.
My lily love hath rosy worth!
    Like to a happy flower she clings!
Glories have come up in his eyes—
Wrapt in a fire he leaps, he flies . . .
    Not for himself the lover sings.

In every loveless lane or way
    Hearts have been heavy, prison-cold:
For all who only moan and pray
    Still doth he sing—he sang of old,
Joy-bearer, bard of better things:
Not for himself the lover sings:
    Singer of Summer uncontrolled.

Mourners move onward from the gloom—
    Not for himself the lover sings:
Give us, they cry, the buds, the bloom,
    The long light on our journeyings.
Star follows star in the dull grey,
Deep is the dark, it drinks the day:
    For very love of God he sings.

The Girl with the Black Hair

HER lips were a red peril
   To set men quivering,
And in her feet there lived the ache
   And the green lilt of Spring.

'Twas on a night of red blossoms,
   Oh, she was a wild wine!
The colours of all the hours
   Lie in this heart of mine.

I was impelled by the white moon
   And the deep eyes of the Spring,
And the voices of purple flutes
   Waltzing and wavering.

Of all the bloom most delicate,
   Sipping the gold air
Was the round girl with round arms—
   The girl with the black hair!

Her breath was the breath of roses,
   White roses clean and clear;
Her eyes were blue as the high heaven
   Where God is always near.

Her lips were a red peril
  To set men quivering,
And in her feet there lived the ache
  And the green lilt of Spring.

'Twas in the Early Summer Time

PERCHANCE it was of Chaucer's day—
    Old Chaucer!—cheerier soul than he
Ne'er drank the good red wine of life,
    And all his rhymes rang joyfully.
Or did it spring from some sad heart—
    A dreamer wandering in the blue,
Who in the slumbering sunlight sang
    Of sweetness that he never knew?
Poor old faint half-forgotten rhyme!
'Twas in the early Summer time.

I dreamed a dream of gardens clothed
    In many a bloom of pink and snow;
Of meadows where a river ran,
    And woodland noises sweet and low:
The bold hills and the great calm sky,
    The song-birds warbling far away,
The green wheat in the ear, and all
    The glory of a golden day:
—Poor old quaint, half-forgotten rhyme!
'Twas in the early Summer time.

I dreamed of kisses and of tears,
    A sweet warm world, and wondrous fair;
Of lovers lingering in the gloom,
    And holy men at evening prayer;
Of singers and their brave old songs,
    Of flowers and many a field of hay,
Of strong men riding out to war,
    And children dancing at their play:
—Poor old quaint, half-forgotten rhyme!
'Twas in the early Summer time.

Five hundred years ago, and more!
    Five hundred years—and I to-day
Am sauntering in the bloom, and lo,
    A sigh! a kiss! they haste away . . .
My heart beats happier for your loves!
    My heart is merrier for your joy!
God's blessings come in sun and bloom
    To every love-sick girl and boy!
—Poor old quaint, half-forgotten rhyme!
'Twas in the early Summer time.

As Far as My Heart Can Go

I CARE not now for the gardens or the gayest flowers that grow:
The little flower in the firelight is as far as my heart can go.

I care not now for the long road o'er the mountains far away;
The little world that we love in is far as my feet can stray.

No smile from me from the city! No salty call for me!
The mouth of my little sweetheart is as far as my eyes can see.

I sing no more of the red wars; I have no love for steel;
The glamour of my darling is as far as my lips can feel.

What can I know of heaven? What should a lover know?
The little face at the fireside is as far as my heart can go.

Her Eyes

DARK eyes are hers; but in their darkness lies
   all the white holiness of Paradise;
A tender violet within them shows
   and the unsullied beauty of the rose;
     Dark eyes are hers.

Dark eyes are hers—that move my heart to sing.
They have consumed the Summer! caught the Spring!
Stolen the star-light, and exultingly
   lifted the moon-beams' old embroidery:
     Dark eyes are hers.

The Hour Is Lost

THE hour is lost. Was ever hour so sweet?
   Fruitful of blessing, friends and honeyed words—
The sunlight in our faces—at our feet
   The world, bright, beautiful, its flocks and herds,
   Foliage of forests, choruses of birds . . .
O happy time, why did we stand downcast?
We should have leapt for love: but now, the hour is past.

The hour is lost. Scarce had we time to mark
   The glory of the green, the sky's soft blue;
It came as silently as comes the dark,
   Our hearts burned hot within us ere we knew . . .
   Then suddenly we said, Can it be true
This golden time was ours?—and now downcast
We stand dumb and amazed. Alas! the hour is past.

Surely God Was a Lover

SURELY God was a lover when He bade the day begin
Soft as a woman's eyelid—white as a woman's skin.

Surely God was a lover, with a lover's faults and fears,
When He made the sea as bitter as a wilful woman's tears.

Surely God was a lover, with the madness love will bring:
He wrought while His love was singing, and put her soul in the Spring.

Surely God was a lover, by a woman's wile controlled,
When He made the Summer a woman thirsty and unconsoled.

Surely God was a lover when He made the trees so fair;
In every leaf is a glory caught from a woman's hair.

Surely God was a lover—see, in the flowers He grows,
His love's eyes in the violet—her sweetness in the rose.

You, and Yellow Air

I DREAM of an old kissing-time
    And the flowered follies there;
In the dim place of cherry-trees
    Of you, and yellow air.

It was an age of babbling,
    When the players would play
Mad with the wine and miracles
    Of a charmed holiday.

Bewildered was the warm earth
    With whistling and sighs,
And a young foal spoke all his heart
    With diamonds for eyes.

You were of Love's own colour
    In eyes and heart and hair;
In the dim place of cherry-trees
    Ridden by yellow air.

It was the time when red lovers
    With the red fevers burn;
A time of bells and silver seeds
    And cherries on the turn.

Children looked into tall trees
    And old eyes looked behind;
God in His glad October
    No sullen man could find.

Out of your eyes a magic
    Fell lazily as dew,
And every lad with lad's eyes
    Made summer love to you.

It was a reign of roses,
    Of blue flowers for the eye,
And the rustling of green girls
    Under a white sky.

I dream of an old kissing-time
    And the flowered follies there,
In the dim place of cherry-trees,
    Of you, and yellow air.

Dear Little Cottage

'TIS not for the lilies, white lilies and tall:
The grass has outlived them, it grows by the wall
   Of the dear little cottage that I know . . .

'Tis not for the cherries—the cherries are wild,
And into their branches has clambered no child
   To drink up the blood of a cherry.

'Tis not for the river, hemmed in by the weir,
Or the lilt of the winds in the glow of the year
   When the birds o' the water make merry . . .

A spell is upon me, and why should I stray
When I have fine company all the long day
   In the dear little cottage that I know.

It is for the voices, the voices that blessed,
The lips that made music, the hands that caressed
   In the dear little cottage that I know.

It is for the shadows that sit by the door,
The feet that go tripping the old broken floor
   At night when the fiddles are shrieking.

It is for the counsel, long-loving and wise,
The hopes that were born in a legion of sighs . . .
   The lips (oh, the cold lips) are speaking.

It is for a temple enshrouded in mist,
A rosy girl raising her face to be kissed
   In the dear little cottage that I know.

Roses Three

WHAT is a rose—a white, white rose?
   A sweetheart sweetening in the Spring:
Shyly she lives, and shyly grows,
   Mourner and mystic—blossoming.

What is a rose—a red, red rose?
   A woman proud, in a proud hour:
Scented of love, she overflows—
   It is the ripening of the flower.

What is a rose, a yellow rose?
   A woman grave, in the pale gold
Braver than all—she smiles and knows
   It is the quiet'ning for the cold.

The Sacrifice

WHITE for the grave, strange-eyed and sable-dressed,
    Is this my love so quietly doth lie?
The sunlight of her sweetness, her dear grace,
    All that she gave . . . falls to the earth to die.
Love's utter sacrifice—life's old long pain—
Lost! lost! and shall this ever live again,
        O, God of pity!

White for the grave—all grace, all glory gone!
    My love was young, my love was sweet and warm,
And so we dreamed as quiet voyagers . . .
    Most hateful wreck! too cruel strife and storm!
The grave will cry its hunger every hour;
Yet thus to spoil the glory of a flower,
        O, God of pity!

Yet in her rest she shall not see gray hairs
    Or children trampling on the holy things;
Though every day be dark, still in the dark
    Love looks for light, the old hope climbs and clings
Up through all tears . . . In the black gloom and pain
My torn heart cries, "Give me my love again,
        O, God of pity!"

Little White Girl

FEARS are mine for a face so pretty!
    Violets perish, lilies are few:
    There is an ache in my heart for you:
In all the tawdry, treacherous city
    You are the one thing white and clean,
    The only riches where all is mean,
Little white girl so pale and pretty!

Fears are mine for a face so pretty!
    I have been lover of lips and chins,
    And a listener to violins
Crying for love and calling for pity;
    And it all comes back with your eyes and hair . . .
    But the darkness threatens you everywhere,
Little white girl, so pale and pretty!

In the Street

THE night, the rain, who could forget?—
The grey streets glimmering in the wet:
Wreckers and ruined wreckage met:
    There was no dearth
Of all the unlovely things that yet
    Must plague the earth.

Gloom, and the street's unhallowed joys:
The sly-eyed girls, the jeering boys:
Faint-carolling amid the noise
    A woman worn—
A broken life: a heart, a voice,
    Trembling and torn.

She did not sing of hillside steep,
Of reapers stooping low to reap:
No love-lorn shepherd with his sheep
    Made moan or call:
A mother kissed her child asleep,
    And that was all.

Slowly into our hearts there crept
I know not what: it flamed! it leapt!
Was it God's love that in us slept? . . .
    I saw the mark
Of tears upon her, as she stept
    Into the dark.

Child of Tears

IMPETUOUS as a wild-winged bird
   Your mother could not be a slave;
Her gift she gave unto the world,
   A child of many tears she gave.

No mouth was mad your mouth to kiss,
   No bosom held you safe and warm,
Poor little soul who came and cried
   And no one heard you in the storm.

The people of the market-place
   Of all your shame made merry play;
The worshippers to chapel went
   And said, Our hearts are clean to-day.

Each mother to her white breast held
   Her little mite of Love's own gold;
Softly she sang for its sweet rest,
   And you were sleeping hard and cold.

They said of you, His eyes are bright;
   Fair was his mother's face to see.
His mother's heart was false and black
   So as his mother he shall be.

Why the dark shadows hovering frowned
    You knew not with your wondering eyes;
You played about the brink of Hell,
    And you were sweet for Paradise.

In the long row your little grave
    Can cover all your baby fears;
The great world cursed you and you died,
    Dear little unloved child of tears.

The Petticoat Plays

TEACH me not, tell me not,
    Love ever sinned!
See how her petticoat
    Sweetens the wind.

Back to the earth she went,
    Broken at noon;
Here is her petticoat
    Flapping a tune.

Have ye not ever heard
    Petticoats sing?
I hear a mourning flute
    And a sweet string.

Little silk ally in
    This her last war,
Know ye the meaning of
    What she died for?

Mourner most delicate,
    Surely you hold
Manna that she has stored
    Safe from the cold.

She had the loving blood,
    Love gave her eyes,
And the world showered on her
    Icicles—lies.

Speak to her, little wind,
    Lovable sky,
Say to the soul of her
    Brava—good-bye.

Teach me not, tell me not,
    Love ever sinned:
See how her petticoat
    Sweetens the wind!

The Loving Tree

THREE women walked upon a road,
    And the first said airily,
"Of all the trees in all the world
    Which is the loving tree?"

The second said, "My eyes have seen
    No tree that is not fair;
But the Orange tree is the sweetest tree,
    The loving blood is there."

And the third said, "In the green time
    I knew a loving tree
That gave a drink of the blood-red milk,
    It was the Mulberry."

Then the first one said, "Of all the trees
    No sweetest can I name;
Ask her who yonder slowly comes—
    That woman lean and lame."

Grief like a hideous suckling hung
    Along her hollow breast,
Pain was upon her as she walked,
    And as she stooped to rest.

"Why will you question so?" she said,
   "Is it to mock at me?
For how should I, who walk in Hell,
   Know of a loving tree?

"My eyes are not as woman's eyes,
   They hope not east or west:
Dull Famine my bed-mate is,
   And Loneliness my guest.

" 'Tis not the most delicious flower
   That leaves the scent of Spring,
Nor is it yet the brightest bird
   That loads his heart to sing.

"A tree may dance in the white weather
   Or dream in a blue gown,
A tree may sing as a sweetheart
   To bid the stars come down:

"Some trees are slim and lovable
   And some are sleek and strong,
But the tree that has the cripple's heart
   Will know the cripple's song.

"The sweetest death is the red death
   That comes up nakedly,
And the tree that has the foiled heart
   It is the loving tree.

"While ever lip shall seek for lip,
    While ever light shall fall,
The tree that has the ruined heart
    Is tenderest of all.

"Oh, ye may have your men to kiss,
    And children warm to hold,
But the heart that had the hottest love
    Was never yet consoled."

The women three walked on their way,
    Their shamed eyes could see
How well the tree with the foiled heart
    Is still the loving tree.

Inland Born

THE tall man wooed her in the South,
    They loved along the Sea;
The tall man caught her to the North
    And she went tearfully.

He talked of all the full seasons,
    The white wheat was his gold;
But the long fight in the wilderness
    To her he never told.

She saw the cool brown Winters pass,
    The heart-sick Spring come on,
And the Summer as a great tyrant
    Till half her hope was gone.

Her lips they were the woman's lips
    Eager to bless and blame;
The lean years quelled her, and in them
    Her snow-white children came.

At night she sang them to their sleep
    With cool songs of the Sea,
And in the day her big soft eyes
    Went South eternally.

She sang of boats and merriment,
    And ships that come and go,
Of orchards and the rosemary,
    And all the flowers that grow.

She sang of all the miracles
    That in the South are seen,
Of all the gracious waterfalls
    And all the world of green.

She told them of the blue waters,
    Of all her soul had planned,
Of the crying birds and the seaweed
    And the music on the sand.

She said, These whom I love shall go
    Where the wind is sweet and free,
My little inland children
    Shall wander by the Sea.

The elder was a five-years girl
    With the blue eyes of the mother,
And younger by a year there ran
    A flaxen-headed brother.

The North Wind in his war came out
    And ceased not night and day,
And the little inland children
    Had lost the heart to play.

These two fell ill with a quick fever
   —'Twas in the red ripe weather—
Kind neighbours came with flowers for them
   When they lay dead together.

Oh, that we love goes lightly out:
   The clouds play in the sky,
And half the winds say openly:
   Here is a day to die.

Slowly she saw them, and her eyes
   Went South eternally:
She said, God stole my children—
   They never saw the Sea.

An old man said, Your children now
   Shall walk the streets of gold;
But she said, It is a dim Heaven
   And merciless and cold.

Then spoke to her an old mother
   Of Love that is Divine;
But she said, The God of Love he is
   A foe to me and mine.

Then spoke to her a sweet neighbour
   Of good days yet to be;
But she said, God stole my children,
   They never saw the Sea.

The tall man spoke in lover talk
    To blind her for the day,
But the Sunlight was more merciful:
    It had no word to say.

The Child We Lost

SIX weeks it was till Christmas time
    And Summer seemed not far away;
The white sheep ran upon the hills,
    The white lambs bleated all the day:
Oh, never was the earth more fair!
There was a sweetness in the air
That sang of heaven everywhere.

The garden was a world of bloom;
    The cherry-trees were red and green;
A league away the white smoke rose—
    And always did there come between
The glory that we feel and know
When sunlight seems to overflow
Into a green, warm world below.

Our brown-eyed beauty claimed a kiss:
    Sweet were her words, and full of play:
Light as the dancing thistle-down
    Was all her airy talk that day—
Of flowers, and skies, and heavenly things,
And sometimes softest whisperings
Like music trembling on the strings.

Life to the child was very fair,
    Up from the ranges far and blue
The sun came rosily each morn
    To shine upon the world she knew:
—It was the time when bush-birds sing
And children's thoughts go wandering;
When Summer-time makes love to Spring.

The seasons sixteen times had turned—
    Gladsome or bitter, dark or fair—
Since to our lives there came a love,
    A joy that lightened every care . . .
We watched her wandering down the hill:
We watched her lovingly until
She seemed like someone standing still.

The angels spoke not that bright day:
    Alas, that they should love the gloom!
Had they but whispered, she had turned
    Back to the well-loved garden bloom . . .
O, gentle heart so soft and kind!
O, big brown eyes so bright and blind!
What was it that you sought to find?

. . . Back in the dim, grey times they tell
    Of children tempted far away
In the white flimmering of the moon,
    In twilight or at dawn of day . . .
One evening when the sun was down
A woman came; her eyes were brown.
But our child came not from the town.

Under a Kurrajong

HERE is the ecstasy
   Of sun-fed wine and song:
Drink! it is melody
   Under a kurrajong.

What sweeter space on earth
   For glistening youth and maid
To find the quiet mirth
   Under the quiet shade?

What sweeter place than this
   For loving eyes to see,
For lovers' lips to kiss
   Under the lovers' tree?

It is the time to blow
   Hot kisses on the Spring,
When dreams begin to go
   Under the blossoming.

Let not the mouth be cold:
   Love is not over-long:
Only to-day is gold
   Under a kurrajong.

The Luckless Bard to the Flying Blossom

YOU and I and our kind
    Had glees together:
Now in our turn shall we find
    Foul friends and weather.
You had the love of the sky,
    All the world's honey:
You are a pauper—and I,
    I have no money.

Back in the days that we knew,
    Oh, idle fellow!
You had the heart for the blue,
    The mouth for the yellow:
You who have scented the sky,
    Sat around honey,
You are a pauper—and I,
    I have no money.

In the dim place where we go
    No sweet rebelling
Burns: for the eyes never glow
    Down in our dwelling.
I had the taste of the wine,
    You of the honey,
Little white kinsman of mine!
    I have no money.

From a Coffin

WRAPT in the yellow earth
   What should I fear?
Sour hate and shallow mirth
   Never come near.
Shape me no epitaph!
   Sugar no rhyme!
I had the heart to laugh
   Once on a time.

All the World's a Lolly-Shop

LIFE is behind the counter, and
    he waits on all who buy;
He has a sweet for every mouth,
    a smile for every sigh;
And 'tis the greatest miracle
    that ever did befall—
He has so many customers and
    yet he serves them all.

Now, some do fear too much the powers
    that would all joy retard;
And some bite slow and gingerly,
    and others quick and hard;
And some look ever left and right
    and some have little care—
For all the world's a lolly-shop
    and always trading fair.

Life is behind the counter, and
    he knows not how to frown;
His talk is of a lad's delight
    and of a wench's gown:
He puts the hot love on the lip,
    the red blush on the skin,
And ever to his spacious shop
    the customers come in.

But when the sweetness leaves the sweet
    and sugars bring no joy,
May we have love of tenderling—
    some gracious girl or boy;
And when we have not heart to love
    we are not wanted then,
So let us die as ladies calm
    and courteous gentlemen.

When we shall face the weather bleak
    outside the trembling wall,
Can we be sure of taste of bliss
    or any shop at all?
So let us not despise the place
    where we had feastings rare,
For all the world's a lolly-shop
    and always trading fair.

It Is the Last

WHITE is the world, the weather warm and sweet,
      But time is dear
To thee and me, my friend! for we may meet
      Just once a year.

Soon shalt thou rest, a warrior home from war:
      It seems not strange:
Gently Time maketh thee more ready for
      The old sharp change.

Thou hast done well indeed to come thus far,
      Cheery and bright,
Bold as a tranquil summer evening star
      Smiling good-night.

Thou hast beheld the sunlight, sung the song,
      Fought with the fears,
In the grim days thou hast been all along
      The track of tears.

Thou art not teased of love, afraid of fate
      Or storms within;
Too weary art thou now for hope or hate,
      Small strife or sin.

Still is thy talk of olden time and friend
      That thou hast known;
But all thy stories run to one sad end—
      "I am alone."

How goes the time, O friend of mine? I think
      Thy voice doth fail.
Here is my best tobacco; let us drink
      This good brown ale.

Smoking, I watch thy fainting features through
      The smoky way . . .
O, ancient friend! shall I clasp hands with you
      Next Christmas Day?

The White Flowers Came

'TWAS in the sweet month, tremulous
    With dancing joys that none may quell,
The white flowers came upon the world:
    They taught the old-time parable.

Life looked so very sweet a thing:
    The watcher wept, the lights burned low:
He moved, he felt the long cold kiss
    And yet it seemed not good to go.

Two damsels, underneath the stars,
    Lay listening on the cool green ground:
Faint as the falling dew they heard
    The song that spins the world around.

Strange bickering rose where Death and Life
    Sat quarrelling on the green hillside . . .
Soft as a blessing spoke the bells,
    Blue sky and blossoms for a bride.

Toiling and tired at close of day
    A thin white widow woman prayed . . .
In many a lighted town was told
    The mystery of man and maid . . .

'Twas in the grey of eventime,
    Cool earth and sky delightsome mild,
God's pity came . . . In tears he saw
    The blue eyes of a little child.

The Wedding in September

THEY talked as neighbours solemnly
    Of lambs and wheat and wool . . .
The stripling said, " 'Twill not be dark:
    To-night the moon is full."

Into the wedding feast there came
    The many psalms of Spring:
The fiddler by the seamstress sat
    And said not anything.

The bridegroom was the happiest man
    That ever stepped the town;
But the little seamstress she had cried
    And made the wedding gown.

Oh, ask me not why she has cried!
    Nay, ask a simpler thing:
Why do the little birds go out
    To meet the kiss of Spring?

In with the dark the dancing came
    In a little yellow room,
And by the flowers the old folks said
    The young ones love the bloom.

The fiddler was a witless man
    By night or noon or day,
But the world had need of moistening
    And he had tears to play.

He played the darkness into death
    And stood where joy had been . . .
The bridegroom could not see the bride
    Or know what love could mean.

He played of maids and merriment
    And the young blood of the rover;
Of sacraments he played, and tolls,
    And the baby joy of clover.

The fiddler was a handless man
    That could not sew or reap:
He did not know the care of kine
    Or the many ways of sheep.

Of water-birds he played and boats
    And the white legs in a stream,
Of hot love in the market-place
    And the spinning of a dream.

He played for timorous worshippers
    Who have no God to call;
He played to make the flowers grow,
    To make the manna fall.

He played of falls and holiness
    And the whistling of a rover;
Of sacraments he played, and tolls,
    And the baby joy of clover.

The fiddler played. On lies or hate
    He would not waste a tune:
A bridesmaid pale with jealousy
    Was patient as the moon.

The seamstress had the unsoiled heart
    That suffers heat and chill,
And God had plagued her in the eyes
    With pity hot to spill.

He played of all that men call death,
    Too dear a thing to end:
And Life, the unfilled reveller
    That has a coin to spend.

He played of deeps and loneliness
    And the whistling of a rover,
Of merriment he played and maids
    And the summer-time in clover.

The Hour of the Parting

SHALL we assault the pain?
    It is the time to part:
Let us of Love again
    Eat the impatient heart.

There is a gulf behind
    Dull voice and fallen lip,
The blue smoke of the mind,
    The gray light on the ship.

Parting is of the cold
    That stills the loving breath,
Dimly we taste the old
    The pitiless meal of Death.

The Song and the Bird

HE hath his Heaven got:
    For Love he shakes the tree:
Happy he heedeth not
    The many gods that be.

He telleth all his mad
    Manoeuvring to the morn:
The shy slow-footed lad
    Hears him, and is forlorn.

And doth he grieve or think
    In dreaming drab and dim?
Can aught of dull earth sink
    Into the heart of him?

He fears not wind or sky:
    He counts not moon or year,
Or the many men who die,
    Or the green wheat in the ear.

He knoweth the false and fair
    And the deeps of deep things:
—How shall I know this bird
    Who sings and sings and sings?

The Scent o' the Lover

I SAW the mushrooms hoping
    In the cool June:
It is the scent o' the lover
    Sweetens the tune.

May the good men mock me
    That I dare to say
I have seen buds at kissing
    On a holy day!

'Tis no unsalted music
    The moons bestow,
'Tis the untaught eternal
    So long, so low.

Time is the old man crying
    Lives on a string,
In the eyes of a child fallen
    We fear the Spring.

I am assailed by colours
    By night, by day:
In a mad boat they would take me
    Red miles away.

Love is the loud season:
    Tears fall too soon:
It is the scent o' the lover
    Sweetens the moon.

At the End of Spring

PUT down thy bonny head,
   This is the end:
Thou wert a joyous love,
   Thou wert a pleasing friend:
Soft-silken is the grass
   Where thy twinkling colours blend.

Bend low thy bonny head
   This last sweet morn:
An eager amber child
   Smothered in flowers and corn
Waits for thy death to wear
   The glories thou hast worn.

Bend low thy sunny head:
   Upon the wing
The tender-tinted hours
   Make merry journeying;
The tyrant Sun who slays
   He waits for every Spring.

Bend low thy weary head:
    Kiss all good-bye—
Thy life it was a time
    Of love for lip and eye:
The grief is at our hearts
    That our beloved should die.

For a Child

INTO your angel mouth
   The sport of Spring
And the Summer's honey
   Came rioting.

Your eyes were as flowers,
   Fine gold your hair,
Warm in my heart you sang
   Love like a prayer.

The sunbeam, the moon-mist
   Were one with you,
And all the sighing bloom
   That takes the dew.

Love was about you,
   Through your silken skin
Love like a sun-ray
   Ran out and in.

Wild kiss and heavy love
   Lose every hold,
Oh, sunlight—my sunlight—
   How dark the cold.

The Dream Is Deep

SING me the song that never dies,
   Of little Love blinded and bold,
Blossoms unblemished and blue skies
   And the green going into gold.

All the uproarious pipes we played!
   Frenzy and Folly, Fire and Joy:
Carols we caught up for a maid
   And ballads boisterous for a boy.

I hear the blended bells and bands,
   The fiddlers fiddling on the green,
The clapping of a thousand hands,
   The trembling of the tambourine.

O, happy hours! run kindly slow:
   Black lies the Night, nauseous and grim
Who knoweth what a man may know
   "Not all he hath shall die with him."

The man God made he dreameth deep
   Down in his heart. High in the air
His heaven lies. How shall he sleep?
   He had a dream—the dream was fair.

The Quarrel with the Neighbour

CLEAR was the morning
   ('Twas the time o' the hay)
The little birds running heard
   All we could say.

The quarrel came so quickly
   ('Twas a sweet sunshine),
'Twas the straying of cattle,
   His rights and mine.

Then spoke we fury
   In the white morning air,
—Never again to my doorstep
   Should his body dare.

And he with his big eyes
   By the Great God swore
Never again should my feet
   Come in at his door.

Then did the blood-rush
   Beset me, and I
Told of good I had done him
   In the years gone by.

In his eyes' glitter
   Vile threats could I see,
And he spoke of past favour
   In the old days to me.

'Twas a clear morning
   In the time o' the hay—
With a shut fist my neighbour
   Rode grimly away.

At the end o' the harvest
   Sickness burned me,
Yet always of my neighbour
   I thought bitterly.

Oh, the night—the hot anguish—
   The poor fight with pain;
But I craved not for my neighbour
   At my door again.

'Twas morning. The sunlight
   Ran round at the door.
The voice was an old voice
   Long loved before.

In came my neighbour,
   Shook me by the hand—
He smelt of the morning,
   He smelt of the land.

Of markets and weather
   He spoke cheerily,
And I saw his big eyes
   Look squarely at me.

Of my little sickness,
   Of men we had known,
Of old folk gone under,
   Children all grown.

So spoke we and slowly
   Of days yet to come—
But at his going why,
   Why was I dumb?

When at the doorway
   He laughed Good-bye,
How great was my neighbour!
   How mean was I!

His Love Was Burned Away

SHE seemed as one who looks upon
    a hill and cannot climb . . .
The long days burned her; she was faint
    and white at Christmas-time.

Her lover like a bold spider
    spun lovewebs night and day;
The sunlight knew no pity . . . still
    it burned her blood away.

She died ere yet the butterflies
    knew all her dreamings thin,
She died a blossom penniless
    of honeythirst within.

He talks into the barren night
    that it might hear him pray,
Because it was the long sunlight
    that burned his love away.

He looks as one who sees too far
    and findeth all things dim;
I sometimes think that the deep night
    may blindly pity him.

He will not love the slow delight
    that tells the birth of day,
Because it was the long sunshine
    that stole his love away.

He talks into the heavy night;
    it laughs not as the day;
It dances not as the sunlight
    That stole his love away.

For a Little Girl's Birthday

IS there a beauty over pain,
    Is there of music for a song,
Gentle as sunlight on the rain,
    Gentle with crying all day long?

How should a singer of the cold
    Seeing strange holiness in air
In his blue famine seek to hold
    Vainly your paradise of hair?

Once in a wonderment I prayed:
    —Earth is upon me tedious mild:
Hear me, O hapless God of Aid!
    Throw me a heaven around a child.

When Kisses Are as Strawberries

WHEN bees are hot with honey-thirst
    and hastening with the Spring,
When kisses are as strawberries
    and Love is more than king—

When quiet birds have merriment
    by waters brown and blue,
And little maids wool gathering
    will murmur, "I love you"—

When blossoms dance in carnival
    to hearten maids and men
And kisses are as strawberries
    who would be sober then?

Schoolgirls Hastening

FEAR it has faded and the night:
    The bells all peal the hour of nine:
The schoolgirls hastening through the light
    Touch the unknowable Divine.

What leavening in my heart would bide!
    Full dreams a thousand deep are there:
All luminants succumb beside
    The unbound melody of hair.

Joy the long timorous takes the flute:
    Valiant with colour songs are born:
Love the impatient absolute
    Lives as a Saviour in the morn.

Get thou behind me Shadow-Death!
    Oh ye Eternities delay!
Morning is with me and the breath
    Of schoolgirls hastening down the way.

Dolly's Offering

DOLLY has fashioned a wee bird home—two white eggs in a nest:
I dare not laugh at a holy thing, or a place where the young may rest:
Rude it is, but the mother love in Dolly beats home to me:
It shouts aloud of the heights of love and the wells of its melody.

Lips and eyes in the summer time and the faintest feet are bold:
Colours come to the heart and sing the song that is young and old:
The skies salute and the winds salute and the face of the earth is kind—
But Dolly can never come out to see, for Dolly is lame and blind.

Dolly is wise at eleven years old, for the dark has been her law:
Her body is put in a frozen place that only a love can thaw:
Love is keen in this that her two little hands have wrought for me:
It tells of wooing and joy and pain, and the pulse of the greenery.

I go out where the joys awake and the glistening lovers talk;
Joy is there in the young bird's flight and joy in the young child's talk;
Joys alight with the honey bees at the gates of the honey comb;
But 'tis a piece of the endless dark where Dolly is chained at home.

Dolly is all for love, it speaks in a thousand ways and shrill:
A home she heats with a good red heart, as a woman ever will:
The poor little nest is lined with love as warm as a man may find:
Out of the blackness light is called—and Dolly is lame and blind.

To a Schoolgirl

O MOST unconscious daisy!
   Thou daybreak of a joy!
Whose eyes invade the impassioned man
   In every wayside boy.

Can I, walled in by Autumn,
   With buoyant things agree?
Speak all my heart to a daisy
   If one should smile at me?

Out of the Summer fallen,
   Can I of Summer sing?
Call that I love on the deep yellow
   Between me and the Spring?

'Tis the White Plum Tree

IT is the white Plum Tree
   Seven days fair
As a bride goes combing
   Her joy of hair.

As a peacock dowered
   With golden eyes
Ten paces over
   The Orange lies.

It is the white Plum Tree
   Her passion tells
As a young maid rustling,
   She so excels.

The birds run outward,
   The birds are low,
Whispering in manna
   The sweethearts go.

It is the white Plum Tree
   Seven days fair
As a bride goes combing
   Her joy of hair.

The Unlovely Player

OVER his petty mouth, his sorry chin,
There runs a carnival—a summertime
   of follies men call sin.

What thing is on his soul he will not say.
Come on! come on! ye keen of wit and hear
   the unlovely fellow play.

Playing and loving much, he seems so hot
He could show sweetness to a sunbeam, and
   he would offend it not.

Have ye within your soul so faint a joy?
He will put diamonds on it, though he be
   a dull, grey-headed boy.

His heart hath done a warfare with old Time,
And he moons deep as ballad-maker who
   tracks up a vagrant rhyme.

He hath been long with Summer, and the gold
Of memory props him up to be a man
   and quite defy the cold.

Sweethearts and fools who have the best of day
Come on! come on! ye quick of wit, and hear
   the unlovely fellow play.

The Eleventh Moon

'TWAS in the eleventh moon I went
    wool gathering in the dim,
Near by me was a lover lad
    and the sweetness was on him.

Lightly his eyes went to the east
    and he with joy was dumb,
His sweet love walked a miracle
    out of the moonlight come.

Oh, but he was the fine lover!
    with a lover's thirsting eye:
—When two hearts beat the tune is sweet
    and knows not how to die.

Her laugh it was the rainbow's laugh
    delicious to the land,
And she gave to him for close loving
    her little silken hand.

Her face was made of Summer thought
    joined with the giddy Spring:
Gently I said, O heart, she is
    too heavenly a thing.

The moon did seem as music spilled
    upon her spotless gown,
And at her height of happiness
    the summer tear came down.

Night—and the silence honey-wet:
    the moon came to the full:
It was a time for gentle thought
    and the gathering of wool.

The Evening Is the Morning

TO make my love more delicate
   I say into her eyes
The evening is the morning, dear,
   but in a sweet disguise.
The morning was too loud with light
   and the many birds would sing—
Who but the thoughtless would exchange
   The Autumn for the Spring?

To make my love more beautiful
   I sing into her ear
'Tis not the morning that I love,
   it is the evening, dear:
No sweets of all the sweets we knew
   are sweet as those we know,
And tho' she sighs most heavily
   she says 'tis even so.

I say to make my sweetheart laugh
   now all our work is done,
The evening is the morning dear,
   we shall deceive the sun:
Her hair that once was summer heat
   is but a bloom in gray,
Still she will tell me Evening is
   the Morning that I say.

The Orange Tree

THE young girl stood beside me. I
    Saw not what her young eyes could see:
—A light, she said, not of the sky
    Lives somewhere in the Orange Tree.

—Is it, I said, of east or west?
    The heartbeat of a luminous boy
Who with his faltering flute confessed
    Only the edges of his joy?

Was he, I said, borne to the blue
    In a mad escapade of Spring
Ere he could make a fond adieu
    To his love in the blossoming?

—Listen! the young girl said. There calls
    No voice, no music beats on me;
But it is almost sound: it falls
    This evening on the Orange Tree.

—Does he, I said, so fear the Spring
    Ere the white sap too far can climb?
See in the full gold evening
    All happenings of the olden time?

Is he so goaded by the green?
    Does the compulsion of the dew
Make him unknowable but keen
    Asking with beauty of the blue?

—Listen! the young girl said. For all
    Your hapless talk you fail to see
There is a light, a step, a call,
    This evening on the Orange Tree.

—Is it, I said, a waste of love
    Imperishably old in pain,
Moving as an affrighted dove
    Under the sunlight or the rain?

Is it a fluttering heart that gave
    Too willingly and was reviled?
Is it the stammering at a grave,
    The last word of a little child?

—Silence! the young girl said. Oh, why,
    Why will you talk to weary me?
Plague me no longer now, for I
    Am listening like the Orange Tree.

In the Dim Counties

IN the dim counties
   we take the long calm
Lilting no haziness,
   sequel or psalm.

The little street wenches,
   The holy and clean,
Live as good neighbours live
   under the green.

Malice of sunbeam or
   menace of moon
Piping shall leave us
   no taste of a tune.

In the dim counties
   the eyelids are dumb,
To the lean citizens
   Love cannot come.

Love in the yellowing,
   Love at the turn,
Love o' the cooing lip—
   how should he burn?

The little street wenches,
    the callous, unclean
—Could they but tell us what
    all the gods mean.

Love cannot sabre us,
    blood cannot flow,
In the dim counties
    that wait us below.

Show Me the Song

IT is of Love and lovers—all the old dream in me—
Weary am I of Hate and Pride and its finery:
Summer is soon behind and the Autumn stays not long:
Is it of Love that you sing, sing, sing? Show me the song!

Love is not soiled for all they would sully his pretty name:
Blood that is good and red is on every soil the same:
Love will be loud as the sunlight, quiet as the moon,
Sweet as the sigh of a little child that shall waken soon.

Is there a singer would waste his breath in singing Pride
When little Love can follow wherever a man may bide?
I would be listening, listening, out on the green,
But my heart could never come up to tell that my eyes have seen.

Weary am I of Hate that withers the heart of a man:
I can only dream in a heavy way as a peasant can:
Summer is gone so soon and the Autumn stays not long:
Is it of Love that you sing, sing, sing? Show me the song!

The Woman of Ireland

IT was a woman of Ireland in old days I knew
Being far down was embittered—her little voice grew
Loaded with all the sweet honey and having love too.

So would she sit in the long days and mad to the core
Shrill would she say to her Michael to make his heart sore,
How slow would she say to her Michael, "Now love me no more."

Her man would be telling and telling the things he had told
How she would be always a sweetheart; but never consoled
Was she with the little feet falling down into the cold.

Sometimes she would say that the angels did stay at the door,
And sometimes she spoke to the fairies seen long before.
Then slow would she say to her Michael, "Now love me no more."

How strange it did seem that a woman too weary to sigh,
That a woman should take all her honey to sweeten a lie,
That a woman should call to her lover to let his love die.

She would be thinking too long of the flowers and the dew
And of all striving and loving the young lovers do:
"Ah, sure," she would say, " 'tis a famine up there in the blue."

How often at even come little blue clouds in the sky
And she would be knowing their meaning, would make not a sigh,
But taking up all her sweet honey would call a good-bye.

Long would she sit in the summer, and mad to the core
Slow would she say to her Michael to make his heart sore,
How slow would she say to her Michael, "Now love me no more."

Ride Him Away

NOW that I weary, lad o' my heart,
I will not say that the sun is cold—
The days go heavily, joys depart,
The feet can never be quite so bold—
But you have the eyes . . . and the lights of gold
Run like rivers around the day:
      When I am dead,
      Bound to a bed,
Take my horse, my holiday horse,
      Ride him away!

He will not tarry where grey men halt
And long confer of the coming doom;
But he will loiter (an old-time fault)
In shady place, where summer bloom
And whites and yellows defeat the gloom
While birds speak up to the heat of day:
      When I am dead,
      Heavy as lead,
Take my horse, my holiday horse,
      Ride him away!

He will tarry long where the children play.
The young ears listen to sounds that stir
When we have wandered too far away . . .
The clouds come over, the lights demur,
The red goes into the lavender,
When Love has fallen, oh, who would stay?
      When I am dead,
      Nailed to a bed,
Take my horse, my holiday horse,
      Ride him away!

He may stop and linger at some old tree,
A place of lovers and night come down,
Where grasses listen and flowers agree
Till the moon as white as a wedding gown
Puts her tremour upon a town,
And little lovers have tears to say:
      When I am dead,
      Straight in a bed,
Take my horse, my holiday horse,
      Ride him away!

The Magpie in the Moonlight

GOLD he has poured out and silver on this tent of mine:
He leaves in the last of the moonlight his song without wine.

Sable and snow-white the bird is, and he would define
Love in the leaves to the moon in his song without wine.

Old is the love in his music, and cool to the ear:
His joy is the width of a sorrow, the weight of a tear.

He fails not: the many loud singers he will outshine:
Death he will take into Love in his song without wine.

The Birds Go By

WESTWARD at even ... yet never, never to die!
Surely they live as ever the laugh and the sigh:
After the fight and the fall, the defeat of the pilgrim,
      The birds go by.

No, not for dying like all the sweet flowers are they,
—Flowers giving hope to mankind on their little stay,
Failing only as love fails at the end of the day.

Green earth and water have gladdening out of their cry,
Lifting the eyes of the heart to the height of the sky:
I dream that they bear to the dead the thoughts of the living ...
      The birds go by.

The Sweetening of the Year

WHEN old birds strangely-hearted strive to sing
and young birds face the Great Adventuring:

When manna from the Heaven-appointed trees
bids us to banquet on divinities:

When water-birds, half-fearing each blue thing,
trace the blue heavens for the roving Spring:

When schoolgirls listening hope and listening fear:
They call that time the sweetening of the year.

* * * * *

When schoolboys build great navies in the skies
and a rebellion burns the butterflies:

Sunlight has strange conspiracies above
and the whole Earth is leaning out to Love:

When joys long dead climb out upon a tear;
They call that time the sweetening of the year.

Out to the Green Fields

HERE there is crying, cruelty, every tone:
Cruel is iron, and where is the pity in stone?
The ancient tyrannies tower, they cannot yield:
Let the tired eyes go to the green field!

Flowers are foreigners here, subdued and calm,
Standing as children under a heavy psalm:
My heart is ever impatient of standing so:
Out to the green fields the tired eyes go.

Out where the grasses hasten the resolute heart of man!
Out to the place of pity where all his tears began!
Only down with the young love are the fairy folk concealed:
Let the tired eyes go to the green field.

The leaves have listened to all the birds so long:
Every blossom has ridden out of a song:
Only low with the young love the olden hates are healed:
Let the tired eyes go to the green field!

Green Lover

*"Froggie was caught while crossing a brook:
 A lily-white duck came and gobbled him up."*
 —OLD RHYME.

GHOSTS in plenty about the world
    Step lightly here and there:
They take a trip in the chimney-smoke,
    They cough in an empty chair;
But one I know of, he sets his sail
    When the stars run pale and thin:
He sails away at the flush of Day
    In a curled-up lolly tin.

Long ago did he saunter forth
    When the trees come out to bloom:
Oh, evil luck with the lily-white duck!
    He went to an early doom.
Crossing a brook he was. His heart
    Was hot with love therein:
—Now he sails away at the flush of Day
    In a curled-up lolly tin.

The peacock's colour was on his back
    And great thoughts in his eyes:
He would not care for the slow beware
    Of his mother, old and wise!
He hopped elate; but a pitiless Fate
    As a lily-white duck came in:
—Now he sails away at the flush of Day
    In a curled-up lolly tin.

Sugar is love, and honey is love,
    And that is the reason why
He loves to float in a sugary boat,
    And he makes no moan or sigh:
He puts no curse on a race perverse
    (With nothing to lose or win)
He sails away at the flush of Day
    In a curled-up lolly tin.

If ever you rise when the little flowers
    Come shyly one by one,
Whispering little white thoughts of Love
    And leaning out to the Sun:
When the Laughing Jacks by the river side
    Their comedies begin,
Then a ghost in green is plainly seen
    In his curled-up lolly tin.

The peacock's colour is on his back
    And great thoughts in his eyes:
He is no trader, he has no need
    Of a thousand worn-out lies:
He loses well, and he will not grieve
    For the world or its weight of sin:
—He sails away at the flush of Day
    In a curled-up lolly tin.

Whenever I read of kings and queens
    And knights and ladies fair
Who drank of Life as a goodly cup
    Nor dreamed of a sorrow there,
I know they were driven of Love for Love,
    They fought through thick and thin,
And fell for Love—like the glistening ghost
    In the curled-up lolly tin.

The Dawn is ever a creepy time:
    The Mysteries make it so:
Beauty is broken about the sky
    And into the earth below:
Shadows go out, and stars go out,
    And the Royal Red comes in:
—A lover green is always seen
    In his curled-up lolly tin.

Wise men perish, and old dreams go;
    But many, the great and wise,
Have told the truth to our golden Youth
    That a lover never dies!
His bones may whiten, his dust may go
    Where new worlds would begin:
—And Love prevails: 'tis a lover sails
    In the curled-up lolly tin.

Stony Town

IF ever I go to Stony Town, I'll go as to a fair,
With bells and men and a dance-girl with the
   heat-wave in her hair:
I'll ask the birds that live on the road; for I dream
   (though it may not be)
That the eldest song was a forest thought and the
   singer was a tree.

Oh, Stony Town is a hard town! It buys and sells
   and buys:
It will not pity the plights of youth or any love in
   the eyes:
No curve they follow in Stony Town; but the
   straight line and the square:
—And the girl shall dance them a royal dance,
   like a blue wren at his prayer.

Oh, Stony Town is a hard town! It sells and buys
   and sells:
—Merry men three I will take with me, and seven
   and twenty bells:
The bells will laugh and the men will laugh, and
   the girl shall shine so fair
With the scent of love and cinnamon dust shaken
   out of her hair.

Her skirts shall be of the gossamer, full thirty
    inches high;
And her lips shall move as the flowers move to see
    the winds go by:
The men will laugh, and the bells will laugh, to
    find the world so young;
And the girl shall go as a velvet bird, with a
    quick step on her tongue.

She shall cry aloud that a million moons for a
    lover is not long,
And her mouth shall be as the green honey in
    the honey-eater's song:
—If ever I go to Stony Town, I'll go as to a fair,
And the girl shall shake with the cinnamon and
    the heat-wave in her hair.

To an Early-Flowering Almond

GOWNED as a bride thou art
   Caught with the glow,
Giving with ruddy heart
   Blood to the snow.

Thou hast come in to make
   Dreams to the boy,
Lightly the girl will take
   Omens of joy.

Thou hast the taste of all
   Sweethearts in Spring,
Thou hast come out to call
   Colours to sing.

Low rides the sun above,
   Meek as the moon:
Thou art as moist in love
   As a love tune.

Still as a bride thou art
   In a bride's gown:
See! an uplifted heart
   Beats in a clown.

Those Shaded Eyes

EYES of a damsel
   In the ungoverned Spring
Would send me the long roads
   Adventuring!

Reason the unwelcome
   As a coward cries,
"Look not too long under
   Those shaded eyes!"

Eyes so shaded
   Do me inspire
As the falling water,
   The blue ways of fire.

Full eyes burn over
   The fallen mind,
Bid the dumb utter
   Thoughts to the blind.

Such eyes give dreaming
   Of lights that grew
Flowers on the darkness
   Ere the wind blew.

Eyes so shaded
  To me display
Doves in the white of Heaven,
  Death in his day.

Eyes so shaded
  To me declare
Heights, and the birds loving,
  Hollows of prayer.

Reason the unwelcome
  As a coward cries,
"Look not too long under
  Those shaded eyes!"

But my heart is singing,
  "Oh, the green gown!
The woe . . . the sweet weather . . .
  The tears on a town."

The Blue Wren in the Hop-Bush

HIS home is in the wild hop, in brown and lemon green,
And all the orange followers of gold that come between:
He often says, to mock me, "How slow of soul are you!"
And he puts into the broad sunshine his melody of blue.

The bushman's joke is gentle in long November days:
He fears the blue light of his friend may set the world ablaze;
And the blue friend says, to mock me, "How slow of foot are you!"
And he puts into the broad sunshine his melody of blue.

All children who have seen him are gladder for all time:
He spells Romance and Comedy, his body is a chime;
And he often says to my heart, "How thin of blood are you!"
And he puts into the broad sunshine his melody of blue.

April Weather

HOW long—but, nay! it is not long
   Since we two chirped together:
And, oh! we spoke unwittingly,
   And it was April weather.

The sun did seem as one well past
   All jealousy and fretting,
And as an old man lonesome smiles
   Remembering and forgetting.

The cool wind waited patiently
   For all the sun's delaying,
And, like a fallen player, spoke
   The bitterness of playing.

Tears were upon us; and the pain
   Of all the poor misplanted:
Of famine old and merciless
   And children disenchanted.

The sky came up with chronicles
   Beyond the blue air blowing:
The bitterness of Love lived on,
   And Love himself was going.

How long—but, nay! it is not long
    Since we two chirped together . . .
And, oh! we spoke unwittingly:
    And it was April weather.

The Irish Welcome

ALL the good drinks are unworthy! No food is too fine!
(Though you did hate them, you love them: you cannot decline).
Angels are with you! and ten million fairies and more!
—You will never speak ill of the Irish—you tap at the door!

A handshake can feel like a sorrow—a home like a jail:
When hearts are half-frozen, the elegant book-manners fail:
—Though you be son of the Enemy! black to the core!
You will have all the wealth of the Irish—you tap at the door!

Words are not welcome. 'Tis something too deep and too fine.
'Tis like a fiddle strung up—or the sun in the wine.
A welcome can come like a famine, and leave the heart sore;
But the warmth is all there in the Irish—you tap at the door!

A welcome is red with the summer, and hearty and bold:
'Tis something that drags you in, out of the dark and the cold:
—The saints are not far, you can feel them! The blessings all pour!
The leprechauns caper around you!—you tap at the door!

No matter how humble the table, it cannot be bare:
Of all that would put you to Heaven you take the full share:
You will have all the wealth of all Ireland—what could you have more?
The Irish! they make the world Irish!—you tap at the door!

Colour Yourself for a Man

THE seers may chasten; the fools may bid the
    waters dance uphill;
The seers may sorrow that little of all in the
    world can heed their will:
The hills may fall to the vales, and earth forget
    where the rivers ran:
Listen, Sally! Stifle your woes: colour your eyes
    and lips and hose!
        Colour yourself for a man!

Thirst is Heaven, and thirst is Hell, and every
    fire between;
And Famine is old as the Winter time, and Pain
    is an evergreen:
Thirst is the maker of thieves; so, take every
    colour you can!
—Every glitter about the day: colour your words
    on the tiresome way!
        Colour yourself for a man!

Colour is life and hate and heat and a million
    joys beside:
'Tis vanity keeps the world awake, and the
    wealth in a man is pride:
Thirst is the mother of theft, and theft was old

when the world began:
Listen, Sally! Stifle your woes: colour your
thoughts and eyes and hose!
Colour yourself for a man!

The Hen in the Bushes

CALL me the man seeing
   Too much in air:
Low by the little hen
   Love it is there.

Winds of the Summer,
   The red, the unkind,
Tilt at her motherhood
   Resolute, blind.

As a Queen guarding
   Her jewels so rare,
Patiently all the day
   I see her there.

'Tis the Old Tyrant
   To her body come,
He who will leave us all
   Weighted and dumb.

He the Old Tyrant
   Will many men slay,
He will most gladly
   Burn women away.

He turns the peasant lad
   To the raw soil,
He calls by candle-light
   Slaves to their toil.

He it is urging up
   Cities of sighs;
Who has seen Pity yet
   Enter his eyes?

He it is under
   The war and the moan,
He it is under
   The lies on the stone.

Soon will the thin mother
   With her brood walk;
Keen is the crow—and keen,
   Keen is the hawk.

Call me the man seeing
   Too much in air . . .
Low by the little hen
   Love it is there.

The Moon Was Seven Days Down

"PETER!" she said, "the clock has struck
  At one and two and three;
You sleep so sound, and the lonesome hours
  They seem so black to me.
I suffered long, and I suffered sore:
  —What else can I think upon?
I fear no evil; but, oh!—the moon!
  She is seven days gone."

"Peter!" she said, "the night is long:
  The hours will not go by:
The moon is calm; but she meets her death
  Bitter as women die.
I think too much of the flowers. I dreamed
  I walked in a wedding gown,
Or was it a shroud? The moon! the moon!
  She is seven days down."

"Woman!" he said, "my ears could stand
  Much noise when I was young;
But year by year you have wearied me:
  Can you never stop your tongue?
Here am I, with my broken rest,
  To be up at the break of day:
—So much to do; and the sheep not shorn,
  And the lambs not yet away."

"Peter!" she said, "your tongue is rude;
    You have ever spoken so:
My aches and ills, they trouble you not
    This many a year, I know:
You talk of your lambs and sheep and wool:
    —'Tis all that you think upon:
I fear no evil; but, oh! the moon!
    She is seven days gone."

"Peter!" she said, "the children went:
    My children would not stay:
By the hard word and the hard work
    You have driven them far away.
I suffered, back in the ten years
    That I never saw a town:
—Oh! the moon is over her full glory!
    She is seven days down!"

"Woman!" he said, "I want my rest.
    'Tis the worst time of the year:
The weeds are thick in the top fallow,
    And the hay will soon be here.
A man is a man, and a child a child:
    From a daughter or a son
Or a man or woman I want no talk
    For anything I have done."

"Peter!" she said, "'T was told to me,
    Long back, in a happy year,
That I should die in the turning time
    When the wheat was in the ear;
That I should go in a plain coffin
    And lie in a plain gown
When the moon had taken her full glory
    And was seven days down."

Peter, he rose and lit the lamp
    At the first touch of the day:
His mind was full of the top fallow,
    And the ripening of the hay.
He said, "She sleeps,"—but the second look
    He knew how the dead can stare:
And there came a dance of last beauty
    That none of the living share.

How cool and straight and steady he was:
    He said, "She seems so young!
Her face is fine—it was always fine—
    But, oh, by God! her tongue!
She always thought as the children thought:
    Her mind was made for a town."
—And the moon was out in the pale sky:
    She was seven days down.

He sauntered out to the neighbour's place
    As the daylight came in clear:
"The wheat," he said, "it is filling well,"
    And he stopped at a heavy ear.
He said, "A good strong plain coffin
    Is the one I am thinking on."
—And the moon was over his shoulder:
    She was seven days gone.

The Flight of the Weary

YOUR feet have been made for the fairies:
    Your seventeen sorrows are there:
The moonlight has been with the sunlight
    And both have misgoverned your hair:
You love not the noise of the city:
    You love not the scent of the sea;
And, oh, you are weary! how weary!
    And the world is so weary with me.

You cannot go out to the blossom:
    You cannot contend in the play:
I call you the little white maiden,
    The moon that is out all the day.
The lights in the leaves are of scarlet,
    The colour that comes to redeem:
The winds are all painted with honey,
    And we can escape in a dream.

In moods of unmeasured magenta
    The sun has apparelled the day:
The leaves are as words in a fable
    Or tears that come out in a play:
Oh, you with a year to a sorrow!
    The cynical Summer and Spring
Shall both be ashamed of their dancing,
    And you shall hear many birds sing.

Oh, we have been sorry and soiled by
    The low-living scent of the sea:
Come, let us escape in the scarlet!
    And you can be weary with me.
The flowers shall have all the sweet voices
    That ever came into the ear,
And Spring as a mourner shall listen,
    And Summer shall save us a tear.

Out there in beloved October,
    Then shall we anoint for a king
Some little old desolate dreamer
    Who had not the passion to sing:
The wind shall be sweet as the kisses
    That come when a maiden is kind:
The dews out of Heaven shall hasten
    And open the eyes of the blind.

The silent shall speak, and the ears of
    The deaf shall be shaken with sound:
There shall be a forest, and lovers
    Shall make it the holiest ground:
The sunlight shall be with the moonlight
    And leave the delight on your hair:
The birds of the forest shall journey
    And sing the sweet hymns for you there.

The lakes shall be many and gentle:
    The water-birds, holy and wise,
Shall put the grief out of your shoulders
    And pull the pain out of your eyes:
Our God shall be drowsy, and think out
    His thoughts like a beautiful tree;
And you shall be weary! how weary!
    With all that is weary to me.

Love in Absence

WHEN thou art gone but a little way
    I am in a cold fear:
The day like a long sickness is,
    And I count the moon a year.

When thou art gone but a little way
    I am in a deep alarm:
I cry, Oh God! her dear body,
    If it should come to harm!

When thou art gone and light is gone
    I fiercely wish thee near:
The day like a long sickness is,
    And I count the moon a year.

Now mournfully I dream I fall
    Where uncouth shadows be:
I foot it on the mist,—the heart
    Renounces liberty.

The Child Being There

SHE will be looking at all the bright shops in the town,
Some like the sunrise, and some like the sun going down:
—"Such lights," she says, "are in Heaven. Oh, that I might stare
Right in through the door into Heaven!—my child being there."

She being so long a great sinner—ill-spoken—unwise—
Softly she goes now, and looking at God with both eyes;
And she will say at the midnight—her heart lying bare—
"Surely I have part of Heaven?—my child being there."

Loneliness hangs on her dress—it is now the long worn:
On the shoes that are broken—the hat that has fallen forlorn:
She says: "Would God see me, I wonder now? if I should stare
Right in through the door into Heaven—my child being there."

She will be looking at women the young and the strong,
And the frocks of the little ones laughing and dancing along:
" 'Tis hard that they have all the riches!" she says in despair:
"I helped in the making of Heaven—my child being there."

Poor though her body be, still it is goaded of Love:
—This that can hasten the tiger, and moan with the dove:
This that can make God a shadow. She says: "I will dare!
I will look for a moment in Heaven!—my Child being there."

He Sold Himself to the Daisies

HE stayed too long in the sunlight,
   He was so thin and shy,
He sold himself to the daisies
   When no one strove to buy.

They called him hopeless coward,
   They called him dull and mean,
Because he spoke to the people
   His elders had not seen.

Slow were his eyes and only
   The dull speech on his tongue,
He sold himself to the daisies
   When a summer day was young.

For the daisies came together,
   And they made no boastful sound,
And the grasses fell as playmates,
   Over the green ground.

The traders knew no pity,
   They called him shapeless clown,
And they put long prayers upon him
   And chained him in a town.

But he rose ere the day had broken,
    He rose when the stars hung high,
And his heart did hope within him
    To die as the daisies die.

The daisies climb together,
    They meet not death alone,
Their only life is loving
    And the daisies know their own.

They make no changeless Heaven,
    No God with a furious Law,
And the dreamer under his eyelids
    Saw that the daisies saw.

The traders saw him loiter
    (And he had small heart to toil)
They said he was born to evil,
    A black weed on the soil.

The clouds came thick and thicker,
    The blue winds one by one
Baffled his hopeless body,
    Carried him out of the sun.

They gave to him small pity
    Of priest or prayer or stone,
But the daisies climbed together
    And the daisies knew their own.

So Sweet a Mouth Had She

HER eyes foretold of happiness
    As grapes foretell of wine:
Her feet were as the lights that fall
    In greeneries divine.

Her forehead seemed a clear heaven
    Where all the loves agree:
Her lips were as the flowers' lips,
    So sweet a mouth had she.

Her hair was like the thoughts that fall
    As raiment for a rhyme:
Her bosom was a white morning
    In the keen Summer-time.

She had that old delightsomeness
    Shed by the strawberry,
And lacked not kisses in her time—
    So sweet a mouth had she.

Lament for Early Buttercups

THE lambs are white and lavender, the frost is with the moon,
The mushrooms go to God and say they cannot die so soon:
Oh, they would see the love-works of the birds sent up to sing!
And I—I mourn for buttercups that stay not till the Spring.

Oh, that they were adventuring in long November days
When barley-tips are in the dance to every wind that plays,
When old birds lose all that they love and young birds feel the wing:
I mourn—I mourn for buttercups that stay not till the Spring.

Oh, had their gold delayed until the last moon of the year
When maids bedeck themselves and say that princes will appear,
They would have loved with a warm love the birds sent up to sing:
I mourn—I mourn for buttercups that stay not till the Spring.

Half a Life Back

HALF a life back now the faces careworn or sunny,
  Stare as we knew them, patient with heavy good-byes;
Yet they give still the good warmth and the taste of the honey:
  Neighbour! oh, neighbour! the light has gone out of their eyes.

Did we despise them?—We made little room for their sorrow:
  All that was truth to them seemed to us spotted with lies:
They did so steadily speak of a shining to-morrow:
  Neighbour! oh, neighbour! the light has gone out of their eyes.

Ruddy men, sallow men, praying and ever rebelling:
  Men with their dreams burning out—women unwise—
To little white overloved children parables telling:
  Neighbour! oh, neighbour! the light has gone out of their eyes.

The Lad Who Started Out

OCTOBER and the shining air put wondrous thoughts in him;
And he could fight and climb and ride, and he could shoot and swim:
The baby was about him yet, but a mystic fever ran
In the little lad who started out one day to be a man.

Tempting and fair, two furlongs off, there rose the forest green
Where the subtle bees had hid their home; but the river ran between.
Out of a gaudy dandelion a whispering pirate flew,
And the fever spoke in the dear lad and told him what to do.

Ay, 'twas a madness of the heart! but of the kind that goes
With the kingly men and conquerors, wherever red blood shows:
A thousand fathers stormed in him and drove him in his dream;
Quickly he cast his clothes aside and walked into the stream.

The babe's blue was on his eye, and the yellow on his hair:
Proudly he held the good broad chin that all the heroes bear:
But oh! too high and far and strong the snow-fed river ran
For the little lad who started out one day to be a man.

* * * * *

Ah, madly comes the taste of him in coats the children wear,
And the red caps of the toddlers, and ruddy legs and bare:
The pirates whispering in the gold say grievous things of him,
And the leaves along the sunshine laugh, because he could not swim.

There is a woman sweet and kind, a woman calm and grey,
And her eyes have love for little lads in all their boisterous play.
She says, "So was his merry heart! so was his pretty chin!
My sorrow must run out and out, for I dare not keep it in."

But when the snow-fed waters come, and the yellow's in the air,
She looks not long on the blue sky; for his blue eyes are there:
Oh, the yellow had not left his head when all her tears began
For the little lad who started out one day to be a man.

To a Lodging-House Canary

IN you are all the good jigs of the Irishman out for a day,
Little one! close to the Maker you whistle away.

Prisoned, and born in a prison, and yet in your song
Out to the top o' the twilight you take us along.

The goodman has need of sweet noises; he calls to his dame:
And she, being barren, she knows but the edge of the flame.

You dance into heaven, O rude one!—and higher and higher
You mock at the craven who eats not his fill o' the fire.

Free men we are not: we cannot come out of the fear.
Call the dead! Let the dead march in your merriment here!

Soldier you are, and good neighbour: you come not to cry
Of any dull ache in the body or doubt in the sky.

In you are all the good jigs of old Irishmen out for a day,
Little one! close to the Maker you whistle away.

Native Companions Dancing

ON the blue plains in wintry days
    These stately birds move in the dance.
Keen eyes have they, and quaint old ways
On the blue plains in wintry days.
The Wind, their unseen Piper, plays,
    They strut, salute, retreat, advance;
On the blue plains, in wintry days,
    These stately birds move in the dance.

Stephen Foster

(Composer of "My Old Kentucky Home")

WHO was the man? he was not great or wise,
   He lived in sore distress,
Always he went with pity in the eyes
   For burnt-out Happiness.

He who was poor had melodies of gold,
   He had the rude man's Art,
No one can now deny him—he could hold
   The quick roads to the heart.

The Stolen Lament

IT has the seal of sorrow; it was born
In lamentation where sweet women died
And the red smoke came out upon the corn.

Leave it in pity—it is sealed of woe—
Lest you should hear the hisses of the Dead
Of Ireland seven hundred years ago.

Beauty of light is on it, scent of dew
That once in Heaven was, the bud that came
On trees of happiness that never grew.

Beauty it has that never came by words,
The lordly evidence of Summer-time,
And the deep adoration of the birds.

It has been lifted on rebellion's red.
But listening in the calm we know that night
Is but a generous playtime for the Dead.

* * * * *

Its wealth of tears is not for you to know,
Lest you should hear the hisses of the Dead
Of Ireland seven hundred years ago.

The Whistling Jack

NOT far above me in the boughs he sat, a solemn thing;
On the grey limb in grey he sat, he did not move to sing:
He was so dumb, he seemed to see no glamour in the Spring.

Near by me did the chickens run beneath their mother's eye:
'Twas but a little noise I heard, and I looked up to the sky—
The Whistling Jack and a white chicken! I did not see it die.

He ate so greedily, and then—as if he did no wrong—
He poured into the morning air the beauty of his song:
And I stared at him, I scowled at him: I kept not silence long.

"This is," I said, "no little thing. How can you live and dare
To sing this song that is a song, and sometimes is a prayer?
And the blood is still upon your beak, and tells of murder there.

"When the mother at the even-fall will, with the mother wing,
Give love unto her brood, and they in eager love will cling:
What of the blood upon your beak? Is it a little thing?"

The Whistling Jack hopped lower down, and he looked me in the eye.
He said, "I kill to eat; but you pray long into the sky
For the help of God in all you do, to make your fellows die.

"I know not God. How could I? But I am not always dumb;
With many flags you march: you make strange noises on a drum;
And you praise God for murders old, and murders yet to come.

"Your hymn you found with mating birds; and you have stolen prayer:
All earth you claim and all the sea, and even the sweet air;
You, without pity, cry to God for all His love and care.

"Your Heaven is but a theft; you saw the white walls in the sky;
And the mystery of the wings you took to make your angels fly:
For all your bravery as a thief—you have not loved to die.

"You own the earth and all therein, and all you hear and see:
You cut the flower into the heart, your axe is at the tree;
You burn the body beautiful that was a friend to me.

"If this you say to me is true, that slaughter is a sin,
What of the hat upon your head? the shoes you saunter in?
The fur you found by cruelty, by cruelty the skin?

"You have not ceased one day to rob, since ever you were born;
There was a theft to give you milk, and all that you have worn
Is only yours by plunder foul that fills me with a scorn.

"If you can preach of murder, I can preach of murder too.
You have defiled the sweet, green earth, and prayed into the blue
For strength unto your God that you may other murders do.

"I am a little thief; but you with evil caution strive
For the white wool and the glistening silk, and the honey of the hive!
But for a million cruelties you would not be alive.

"Of valour do you boast, and yet your whole life is a whine.
Where is your pity for the sheep? Your mercy for the kine?
You who would dare to preach to me at this little meal of mine!"

This bird had almost stilled my heart, and both my eyes were dim,
There was no mercy in his speech, as I saw him on the limb.
I said, "Perchance he is of God. Who knows the heart of him?"

Oh, the bird he was on fire: he spoke so long and bitterly:
I heard him till at last he flew. I did not wish to see
The heavens blue: for he had put such weakness into me.

The Good Season

THE old mother talks, and her eyes will be dimming and dimming;
    It is the good season that comes up, and, "Oh!" she will say,
"All summer the ducks do I see; they are swimming and swimming!
    The barley it talks to the butterflies wheeling away.

"Oh! that was the season for all the long grass and the clover;
    The oats they were over the fences, and seven foot high!
Our own little creek, it was flooded a dozen times over;
    And water-birds came without warning to blacken the sky.

"But what did we think of? It was not the storing of money;
    For he would be riding to see me the whole summer through;
How sweet was the scent of the world! it was shaking with honey
    And I would be building my palaces up in the blue.

"The sun it was more like a moon; it was never so mellow;
    Your heart would be thinking of plenty, and always at ease;
How drowsy the cattle were! Oh!, and the butter was yellow!
    All summer the little round parrots fell out of the trees.

"The shearing was late; for you never could get the fine weather;
    'Twas close on to autumn the last of the wool was away.
The wheat was too rank, and the year was too rich altogether;
    We started at Easter the second time cutting the hay."

The old mother dreams, and the blood will be thinning and thinning;
    Her eyes they go up to the heavens and over the ground;
She says, "I can see him still, laughing and losing and winning,
    And oh! he looks long at me, riding off, all the year round."

The Soldier Is Home

WEARY is he, and sick of the sorrow of war,
  Hating the shriek of loud music, the beat of the drum;
Is this the shadow called glory men sell themselves for?
  The pangs in his heart they have paled him, and stricken him dumb!
    Oh! yes, the soldier is home!

Still does he think of one morning, the march and the sun!
  A smoke, and a scream, and the dark, and next to his mind
Comes the time of his torment, when all the red fighting was done!
  And he mourned for the good legs he left in the desert behind.
    Oh! yes, the soldier is home!

He was caught with the valour of music, the glory of kings,
  The diplomat's delicate lying, the cheers of a crowd,
And now does he hate the dull tempest, the shrill vapourings—
  He who was proud, and no beggar now waits for his shroud!
    Oh! yes, the soldier is home!

Now shall he sit in the dark, his world shall be fearfully small—
  He shall sit with old people, and pray and praise God for fine weather;
Only at times shall he move for a glimpse away over the wall,
  Where the men and the women who make up the world are striving together!
    Oh! yes, the soldier is home!

Simple, salt tears, full often will redden his eyes;
    No one shall hear what he hears, or see what he sees;
He shall be mocked by a flower, and the flush of the skies!
    He shall behold the kissing of sweethearts—close by him, here, under
        the trees—
        Oh! yes, the soldier is home!

The Poor, Poor Country

OH 'twas a poor country, in Autumn it was bare,
The only green was the cutting grass and the sheep found little there.
Oh, the thin wheat and the brown oats were never two foot high,
But down in the poor country no pauper was I.

My wealth it was the glow that lives forever in the young,
'T was on the brown water, in the green leaves it hung.
The blue cranes fed their young all day—how far in a tall tree!
And the poor, poor country made no pauper of me.

I waded out to the swan's nest,—at night I heard them sing,
I stood amazed at the Pelican, and crowned him for a king;
I saw the black duck in the reeds, and the spoonbill on the sky,
And in that poor country no pauper was I.

The mountain-ducks down in the dark made many a hollow sound,
I saw in sleep the Bunyip creep from the waters underground.
I found the plovers' island home, and they fought right valiantly.
Poor was the country, but it made no pauper of me.

My riches all went into dreams that never yet came home,
They touched upon the wild cherries and the slabs of honeycomb,
They were not of the desolate brood that men can sell or buy,
Down in that poor country no pauper was I.

* * * * *

The New Year came with heat and thirst and the little lakes were low,
The blue cranes were my nearest friends and I mourned to see them go;
I watched their wings so long until I only saw the sky,
Down in that poor country no pauper was I.

The Winter Sundown

THEY falter, they stay not
    To your eyes and mine,
The boatmen in violet
    On bays of wine.

Calm without sorrow,
    The peace without prayer:
All fear is folly in
    That country out there.

Many we mourn are out
    Seaward away;
Tears did they leave us
    As players who play.

The highlands, the hilltops,
    They make the heart bare,
Burned out with wishing for
    That country out there.

* * * * *

They stay not, they stay not,
    But your eyes and mine
Have boatmen in violet
    On bays of wine.

The Bard and the Lizard

THE lizard leans in to October,
    He walks on the yellow and green,
The world is awake and unsober,
    It knows where the lovers have been:
The wind, like a violoncello,
    Comes up and commands him to sing:
He says to me, "Courage, good fellow!
    We live by the folly of Spring!"

A fish that the sea cannot swallow,
    A bird that can never yet rise,
A dreamer no dreamer can follow,
    The snake is at home in his eyes.
He tells me the paramount treason,
    His words have the resolute ring:
"Away with the homage to Reason!
    We live by the folly of Spring!"

The leaves are about him; the berry
    Is close in the red and the green,
His eyes are too old to be merry,
    He knows where the lovers have been.
And yet he could never be bitter,
    He tells me no sorrowful thing:
"The Autumn is less than a twitter!
    We live by the folly of Spring!"

As green as the light on a salad
    He leans in the shade of a tree,
He has the good breath of a ballad,
    The strength that is down in the sea.
How silent he creeps in the yellow—
    How silent! and yet can he sing:
He gives me, "Good morning, good fellow!
    We live by the folly of Spring!"

I scent the alarm of the faded
    Who love not the light and the play,
I hear the assault of the jaded,
    I hear the intolerant bray.
My friend has the face of a wizard,
    He tells me no desolate thing:
I learn from the heart of the lizard,
    We live by the folly of Spring!"

Song for a Honeymoon

THE bells have bidden me speak my heart;
    and the glistening pair I know
Have both defied me to fashion a song to quicken
    them into the glow;
Have both defied me to beckon the words, and
    the folly to feed the tune:
I drop to the shadows, and follow a man, for a
    song for a honeymoon.

The folk I see are a forest folk; their gods go
    everywhere;
They speak their rage on the mountain top; they
    crouch in the golden air;
Their magic lurks in the serpent's eye, in the
    witches' wavering tune;
The Devils of old come down and walk in the
    song for a honeymoon.

The man I see is a barbarous man, but newly
    from the dark;
His spearmen follow him: blood there is wherever
    he leaves his mark.
He tames the leopard; he leads the bull; a lord
    that his slaves obey:
Through burning forests or roaring seas he carries
    a bride away.

This man will have no fear of men; he carries,
he makes the law;
I want the devil about his mouth, and the iron-
stone in his jaw;
And under his shirt the rattle of Life shall beat
so fierce and strong,
Wherever he rides, I too shall ride for the heart-
beat of a song.

The man I see is a resolute man, to a steadfast
    purpose bound;
In pain and hunger he plants the seed, he furrows
    the virgin ground;
He will not flinch in the morning frost, or fail
    in the heat of noon;
I'll follow this man, I need this man, in a song for
    a honeymoon.

The marrow of Life can best be found in a
    brimmed-up fighting man,
Who rules a rabble, who robs a thief, nor cares
    how a fight began;
The sword he rattles; he comes, he owns; a lord
    that his slaves obey;
Through swirling rivers and trackless hills he
    carries a bride away.

The measure of Life can best be found in a
   woman wise and fair,
With peace and plenty about her mouth, and the
   goodwill in her hair;
Whose eyes have courage to strive with Death
   and a thousand fears of old;
Whose pity is clad in a radiance that a million
   tears have told.

Of bells I dream and the merriment, and the
   horseshoe for a sign;
Of the goodly meats, and the honeycomb, and
   the lifting scent of wine;
Of white maids robing and good men's mirth,
   and the great sun on the corn;
Of songs for telling the joys that roll on the day
   that a man is born.

Bells and the blessing—the woman goes with the
   new world in her eyes;
The manna of love has found the Earth, 'tis
   pouring out of the skies;
She knows no famine; her heart is wealth; and
   her patience proud and strong;
The faith in her body, it reigns, it fills, and
   hallows the cradle song.

The man he has builded his first rude home, as
    strong as an eagle's nest;
The woman I see in her early joy, with the young
    life on her breast;
The man and the woman who cheer and guide
    the small feet on the floor
Have found the pity that bids them run to the
    outcast at the door.

I'll borrow the prayers that good men say, and
    the new-born's faintest cry,
The tremor that comes to women and men with
    the sorrow to say good-bye;
And thus will I say to the glistening pair: I have
    sought for a barbarous tune,
I've been on a raid with a right red man, for a
    song for a honeymoon.

The Ballad of Remembrance

I MET a man out Bathurst way in the middle of the year,
He had an honest, kindly face and eyes without a fear;
A pleasant man to look upon and a pleasant man to hear.

And he would talk as men will talk of what their hands have done,
Of plains and hills and the wilderness where sheep and cattle run,
Of the bitterness of frost and rain and the blinding of the sun.

He had the bushman's ready eye, and he heard the faintest sound,
The names he knew of all that flew, or ran upon the ground,
His knowledge was not of the kind that is with scholars found.

One thing I saw whene'er I talked of all red history,
Of England's victories on the land, her strength upon the sea,
He listened quietly, but would say no generous word to me.

The silence of the man was such, that I would more and more
Speak of the English; there had lived never on earth before
A race so just and merciful,—his silence made me sore.

One night I spoke of English law, and what the English do—
"Listen," he said, "and I will tell a shameful thing to you,
'Twas old when I was born, this night it comes up ever new.

"Too long have I been in the bush, my thinking may be slow,
But when you praise the English, then knowing all I know,
If I did not speak, then I should feel the lowest of the low.

"My father, he could fight, although he was but bone and skin,
I saw him fight with a big man, who had the heavy chin,
And the heavy fist. I stood two hours and saw my father win.

"My father had the slow speech, and his words came tenderly;
When we were splitting in the bush one day we took a tree
With young birds in the nest, all day he could not speak to me.

"An open-handed man he was, as all who knew him tell;
He was not hard in anything, he strove to teach us well;
He said. 'There's something in a man, that they dare not buy or sell.'

"My father could not read or write—now little children can,—
Of Death, and things at the back of it, his simple reasoning ran,
And he said, 'I can't believe that God is bitter like a man.'

"How quiet he was, because he stared they said his eyes were dim,
But when he drank, those eyes would change, and his jaws would be so
    grim,
And the thoughts at the bottom of his heart came tumbling out of him.

"'Some things there are,' my father said, 'I keep remembering,
A man's body is coarse, he said, though he may be a king,
But the body of a sweet woman, that is the holy thing.'

* * * * *

"'T was in your England that he starved and he would not dare to kill,
He knew the law, and the law it said, his mouth he must not fill.
All Wisdom came from God, he heard, and the hunger was His Will.

"There was the food before his eyes, and why should he be bound?
The rich men owned each inch of earth and the riches underground;
They would have owned the soul of man had such a thing been found."

"These laws," I said, "were harsh, but they have long since disappeared,
Wherever strong men live and thrive, is English law revered,
That flag is loved, and we are proud to know that it is feared."

But the man he said, "You boast that all the English laws are fair,
Long have I heard such tales, they seem like dust upon the air,
For the English sent my father here for the shooting of a hare.

"One day we were in the deep bush, my father's tongue was free,
I was not far into my 'teens and his back he showed to me,
And even now when I think of it, my eyes can scarcely see."

"These laws," I said, "were cruel laws, they were in every land,
The English gave you all you have and you fail to understand
That laws are made for the English, by the people's own command."

The man he said, "I may be dull, you speak of English law,
Would you so love it had you seen the shameful thing I saw?
For me that back is always bare, those wounds are always raw.

"He was a convict forced to work, when the squatter ruled the land,
For some slight fault his master put a letter in his hand
And he said, 'Take this to Bathurst Gaol, they'll make you understand.'

"Too well the law, my father knew, the law of Lash and Chain,
That day he walked to Bathurst Gaol, 'twas in the blinding rain,
And they flogged his flesh into his bones—then he walked back again."

The man he said, "I have always heard that English laws are fair,
We are a part of England, and her fighting glory share,
But the English sent my father here for the shooting of a hare.

"My father was of England and it is against my will,
Of any nation on the earth, to speak one word of ill;
But I know the English by one mark—my eyes can see it still."

Then spoke I still of England, I would not lightly yield,
"England," I said, "is strong, she does the little nations shield,"
And the man he said, "Some things there are that never can be healed."

The Gentle Water Bird

(For Mary Gilmore)

IN the far days, when every day was long,
Fear was upon me and the fear was strong,
Ere I had learned the recompense of song.

In the dim days I trembled, for I knew
God was above me, always frowning through,
And God was terrible and thunder-blue.

Creeds the discoloured awed my opening mind,
Perils, perplexities—what could I find?—
All the old terror waiting on mankind.

Even the gentle flowers of white and cream,
The rainbow with its treasury of dream,
Trembled because of God's ungracious scheme.

And in the night the many stars would say
Dark things unaltered in the light of day:
Fear was upon me even in my play.

There was a lake I loved in gentle rain:
One day there fell a bird, a courtly crane:
Wisely he walked, as one who knows of pain.

Gracious he was and lofty as a king:
Silent he was, and yet he seemed to sing
Always of little children and the Spring.

God? Did he know him? It was far he flew . . .
God was not terrible and thunder-blue:
—It was a gentle water bird I knew.

Pity was in him for the weak and strong,
All who have suffered when the days were long,
And he was deep and gentle as a song.

As a calm soldier in a cloak of grey
He did commune with me for many a day
Till the dark fear was lifted far away.

Sober-apparelled, yet he caught the glow:
Always of Heaven would he speak, and low,
And he did tell me where the wishes go.

Kinsfolk of his it was who long before
Came from the mist (and no one knows the shore)
Came with the little children to the door.

Was he less wise than those birds long ago
Who flew from God (He surely willed it so)
Bearing great happiness to all below?

Long have I learned that all his speech was true;
I cannot reason it—how far he flew—
God is not terrible nor thunder-blue.

Sometimes, when watching in the white sunshine,
Someone approaches—I can half define
All the calm beauty of that friend of mine.

Nothing of hatred will about him cling:
Silent—how silent—but his heart will sing
Always of little children and the Spring.

www.ingramcontent.com/pod-product-compliance
Lightning Source LLC
Chambersburg PA
CBHW070142100426
42743CB00013B/2805